Creative Slow-Cooker Meals

CHERYL MOELLER

HARVEST HOUSE PUBLISHERS

EUGENE, OREGON

All Scripture quotations, unless otherwise indicated, are taken from The Holy Bible, *New International Version*® *NIV*®. Copyright © 1973, 1978, 1984, 2011 by Biblica, Inc.™ Used by permission. All rights reserved worldwide.

Cover by Dugan Design Group, Bloomington, Minnesota

Cover photo © Dugan Design Group

Cheryl Moeller is represented by MacGregor Literary Inc. of Hillsboro, Oregon.

CREATIVE SLOW-COOKER MEALS
Copyright © 2012 by Cheryl Moeller
Published by Harvest House Publishers
Eugene, Oregon 97402
www.harvesthousepublishers.com

Library of Congress Cataloging-in-Publication Data
  Moeller, Cheryl.
  Creative slow-cooker meals / Cheryl Moeller.
    p. cm.
  ISBN 978-0-7369-4491-5 (pbk.)
  ISBN 978-0-7369-4492-2 (eBook)
  1. Electric cooking, Slow. 2. Cookbooks. I. Title.
  TX827.M64 2012
  641.5'884—dc23
                                                      2011017934

Printed in China

12 13 14 15 16 17 18 19 20 / RDS-SK / 10 9 8 7 6 5 4 3 2 1

To my mother, Gladys Webster,
and to my mother-in-law, Inez Moeller,
who taught me to love cooking.

Contents

INTRODUCTION

Creative Slow-Cooker Meals was born on a "two slow-cooker day" in my kitchen. It was a rainy day and my younger daughters each had a friend over.

"We don't use slow cookers in my house," one little girl said. "My dad says they turn everything into mush."

"They don't have to," I replied. "If you use two slow cookers instead of one, you can make a whole meal without everything tasting the same."

My goal is to show you the same thing. Slow-cooked meals can be healthy and delicious, and are as appropriate for a family meal as a dinner party or potluck.

I come from a long line of amazing cooks. Their recipes were passed down from generation to generation in the kitchen, not on paper. And every one of those recipes has a story. My Grandma Webster, a professional cook, made the best blackberry cobbler I've ever tasted. We knew it was summer when she brought it to the table! My Grandma

and Grandpa Windquist owned a dairy farm, and it just wasn't Christmas without their succulent roast beef. And then there was the popcorn my father would always burn, and the fudge that always came out too hard or too soft, but never quite right. We loved it anyway.

We were all busy with our separate activities when I was growing up—just as busy as your family is today. But when the clock struck the dinner hour, we were all at the table to share our lives. No one questioned this.

My husband, Bob, and I have the same rule with our family of six children (plus the in-laws and grandchildren!). Attendance at family meals needs to be non-negotiable. If missing dinner more than once or twice a week starts to become a common occurrence in our home, we take a hard look at our schedule and cut out whatever it is that's causing us to have "lone rangers" in the family.

Studies show that families who eat together benefit in more ways than one. The dinner table is the place where we come together for heart connections. Sharing a meal will help your children adjust better as teens and adults, converse at a deeper level, become best friends with each other, have a platform for spiritual discussions, and even test better in academics.

Creative Slow-Cooker Meals will help you get the family back to the table while freeing you from long hours spent sweating over a hot stove. Using two slow cookers, you'll have a warm entrée and side dish on the table with hardly any effort! It's my hope that you'll find some recipes here that will become staples in your home, that your family will be telling stories about for years to come. And I pray you will find, as I have, that there are few blessings greater than sharing a meal with family.

10 REASONS TO READ THE DIRECTIONS FIRST

1. Don't fill your slow cooker more than two-thirds full. Foods don't cook correctly if the slow cooker is filled too high. If the food level is lower than this, however, the contents will cook quicker.

2. Cooking for 1 hour on high is equal to 2 hours on low. The low setting on slow cookers is 200° and the high setting is 300°. The minimum temperature for food safety is 140°. Always test for doneness with a thermometer, especially when cooking meat.

3. If there's too much liquid in the dish, you can thicken the juices by removing the lid and cooking on high for the last half hour of cooking time.

4. In most slow cooker recipes, vegetables do not need to be initially sautéed. In almost all instances, ingredients can be added raw at the start and allowed to cook all day.

5. Most meats, except fish, require 8 hours of cooking on the low setting.

6. You will almost always need to coat the slow cooker in nonstick cooking spray before beginning a recipe. As an alternative, most grocery stores carry slow cooker liners. These are plastic bags that you insert into your slow cooker before adding the food. Nonstick spray and liner bags will make cleanup much simpler.

7. Do not set the stoneware liner on a stovetop burner and attempt to heat up the contents. To prevent cracking, never add cold water to a hot slow cooker liner.

8. To avoid heat loss, do not open the slow cooker while cooking except to stir or check for doneness.

9. To avoid curdling dairy products, generally add milk, heavy cream, sour cream, or cheese sometime during the last hour of cooking time.

10. You thought you didn't have a warmer to serve hot food at your next dinner party, but you do, if you own a slow cooker! Your slow cooker also works well as a sorbet maker, fondue pot, pancake and tortilla warmer, rice maker, and punch bowl.

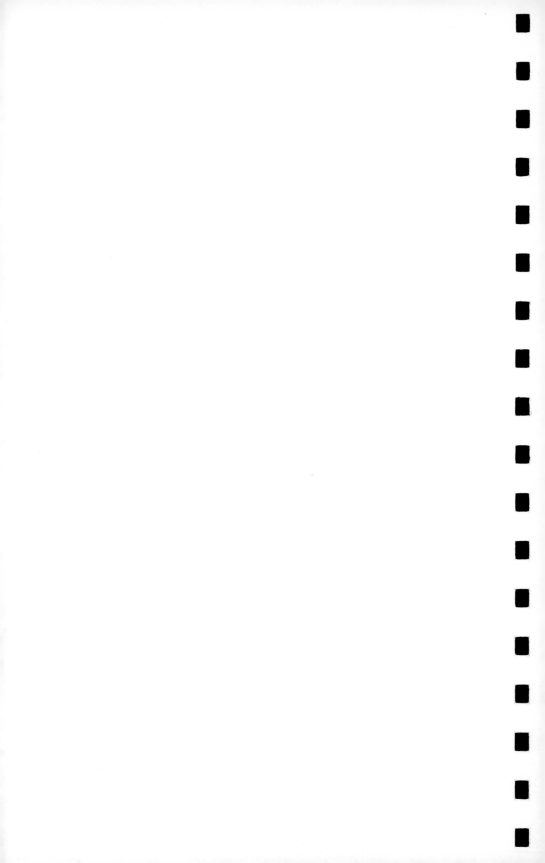

Chapter 1

Take the "Fast" out of Breakfast

*His compassions never fail. They
are new every morning.*

LAMENTATIONS 3:22-23

Overnight Oats
and Triple Berry Oatmeal Topping

Overnight Oats

INGREDIENTS:

1 cup steel cut oats
1 vanilla bean, sliced lengthwise
1 cinnamon stick
5½ cups water

DIRECTIONS:

1. Place all ingredients in slow cooker and stir. Cover and cook on low for 6 to 7 hours.

2. Stir well, then remove vanilla bean and cinnamon stick. Serve with Triple Berry Oatmeal Topping or cream, raisins, and brown sugar.

I love waking up in the morning to a hot breakfast right in my own slow cookers.

Triple Berry Oatmeal Topping

INGREDIENTS:

2 cups strawberries, hulled
2 cups blackberries
2 cups blueberries
2 cups water

DIRECTIONS:

1. Place strawberries, blackberries, and blueberries in slow cooker and pour water over top.

2. Cover and cook on low for 6 to 7 hours. To serve, spoon over Overnight Oats or other hot cereal.

Mulled Apple Cider and Finger Lake Moose Munch

Mulled Apple Cider

INGREDIENTS:

- 1 gallon fresh apple cider
- 1 cinnamon stick
- 4 to 6 whole cloves
- 2 apples, washed and cored
- 2 individual herbal apple tea bags

DIRECTIONS:

1. Add all ingredients to slow cooker and stir. Cover and cook on low for 8 to 10 hours.

2. To serve, strain out cinnamon stick, cloves, apples, and tea bags. Ladle into mugs.

I love drinking apple cider year-round, but it never tastes quite the same out of season. This is a great way to spruce it up! For variety, substitute two pears instead of the apples.

Finger Lake Moose Munch

INGREDIENTS:

½ cup vegetable oil
½ cup real maple syrup
2 tsp. vanilla extract
2 cups 5-minute oats
2 cups bran flake cereal
½ cup sliced almonds
1 cup raisins
1 cup dried cranberries
1 cup dried blueberries
1 cup chopped walnuts

DIRECTIONS:

1. Toss ingredients together in the slow cooker until everything is evenly but lightly coated.

2. Cover and cook on low for 4 hours, stirring once halfway through baking.

3. Let cool completely. Store at room temperature for up to one month in an airtight container.

This is a great "make-ahead" recipe, and I always make sure to keep some Moose Munch on hand! It's delicious with milk in the morning or as a grab-and-go treat on the way to school.

Spinach Asparagus Soufflé and Fruit Kebabs

Spinach Asparagus Soufflé

INGREDIENTS:

- 1½ cups asparagus, chopped
- ¼ lb. spinach leaves
- 4 baking potatoes, peeled and cut into shoestrings
- ½ cup olive oil
- ½ cup shredded monterey jack cheese
- ½ cup shredded swiss cheese
- 1 onion, chopped
- 1 red bell pepper, chopped
- 1 green bell pepper, chopped
- 8 eggs, beaten
- 1 cup half-and-half
- 1 Tbsp. freshly ground black pepper
- 1 Tbsp. seasoning salt

For an exciting variation, you can cook these soufflés in hollowed-out grapefruit rinds! Save the flesh for Fruit Kebabs.

DIRECTIONS:

1. Boil water in a small pot that will fit a steamer basket. Add chopped asparagus to the basket and steam for 8 to 10 minutes. Drain water and transfer asparagus to food processor. Process until asparagus forms a uniform paste.

2. While asparagus steams, lay down a bed of fresh spinach leaves in greased slow cooker.

3. In a separate bowl, mix olive oil and potatoes. Arrange potato mixture evenly on the spinach leaves in the slow cooker. On top of the potatoes, layer the cheeses, onion, and peppers.

4. In a separate bowl, combine the eggs, asparagus paste, half-and-half, pepper, and seasoning salt. Pour egg

mixture over ingredients in slow cooker. Cover and cook on low for 3 to 5 hours.

Fruit Kebabs

INGREDIENTS:

Two pineapples, one whole and one cut into large chunks
1 bunch red seedless grapes
1 bunch green seedless grapes
4 oranges, peeled and sectioned
¼ lb. blackberries
Any other fresh fruit in season
Shredded coconut

DIRECTIONS:

1. Rinse the whole pineapple and place it in the middle of the slow cooker for decoration.

2. Slide pieces of fruit onto metal skewers, making sure to leave a handle for holding. Stick kebabs in the open slow cooker with handle sticking up and out. Cook on high in slow cooker for 1 hour. Do not cover.

3. Pour coconut onto a plate. Remove skewers and roll each kebab in coconut.

This menu is perfect for a Sunday brunch!

South of the Border Breakfast Casserole

INGREDIENTS:

1 dozen corn or flour tortillas
8 eggs, beaten
2 cups milk
2 cups shredded Mexican cheese
1 7-oz. can chopped green chilies
2 large tomatoes, diced
1 red bell pepper, seeded and chopped
1 onion, chopped
1 16-oz. can black beans, rinsed
  and drained
1 cup frozen corn
1 tsp. salt
½ tsp. freshly ground black pepper

> This is delicious served with a side of salsa and sour cream!

DIRECTIONS:

1. Layer 4 of the tortillas on the bottom of greased slow cooker.

2. In a large mixing bowl, combine all remaining ingredients. Pour half the mixture into the slow cooker.

3. Add another layer of 4 tortillas on top of the mixture. Pour the remaining mixture on top, then add a final layer of tortillas.

4. Cover and cook on low for 6 to 7 hours.

Mexican Hot Chocolate

INGREDIENTS:

3 12-oz. cans evaporated milk
4½ cups milk
1 Tbsp. vanilla
1 tsp. nutmeg
½ tsp. chili powder
2 Tbsp. sugar
2 12-oz. bags semisweet chocolate chips
2 cinnamon sticks

DIRECTIONS:

1. Whisk evaporated milk, milk, vanilla, nutmeg, chili powder, and sugar together in slow cooker. Add chocolate chips and cinnamon sticks.

2. Cover and cook on low for 2 to 3 hours, whisking occasionally.

3. Ladle into individual mugs and dust with cocoa powder.

This rich, creamy beverage has just a hint of spice. It's perfect for a chilly morning!

Baked Stuffed Pears
and Maple Sausage Links

Baked Stuffed Pears

INGREDIENTS:

6 large pears
¼ cup dried figs, chopped
¼ cup granola or Finger Lake Moose Munch (see page 15)
1 Tbsp. grated fresh orange peel zest
½ cup water
6 Tbsp. orange juice concentrate
6 mint sprigs

DIRECTIONS:

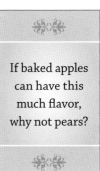

If baked apples can have this much flavor, why not pears?

1. Using a sharp knife or a corer, core each pear, making sure to leave about ½ inch portion of the bottom intact.

2. In a separate bowl, mix together dried figs, granola, and orange peel zest. Stand the pears up in slow cooker and stuff the granola mixture inside. Spoon 1 Tbsp. of the orange juice concentrate over the top of each pear.

3. Pour the water into the slow cooker around the pears in the slow cooker.

4. Cover and cook on low for 3 to 4 hours, or until the pears are tender. To serve, place a mint sprig in the top of each pear.

Maple Sausage Links

INGREDIENTS:

12 sausage links, precooked
¼ cup real maple syrup

DIRECTIONS:

1. Place sausage links in the bottom of slow cooker. Pour syrup over links and stir to coat.

2. Cover and cook on low for 3 to 4 hours.

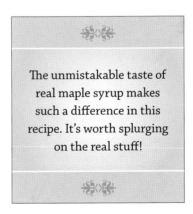

The unmistakable taste of real maple syrup makes such a difference in this recipe. It's worth splurging on the real stuff!

Slow-Cooker Pancake and Basil-Infused Blueberry Topping

Slow-Cooker Pancake

INGREDIENTS:

3 cups flour
2 Tbsp. baking powder
1 tsp. salt
2 Tbsp. sugar
2½ cups milk
2 eggs
6 Tbsp. butter, melted

This is the richest, "cakiest" pancake you'll ever eat!

DIRECTIONS:

1. In a large bowl, sift together the dry ingredients. Make a well in the center.

2. In a separate bowl, beat the eggs and milk. Slowly stir in the melted butter. Pour the milk mixture into the well in the dry ingredients. Whisk until just combined.

3. Pour the batter into well-greased slow cooker. Cover and cook on low for 4 to 6 hours or on high for 2 to 3 hours.

4. Remove cake from slow cooker, slice, and top with Basil-Infused Blueberry Topping.

Basil-Infused Blueberry Topping

INGREDIENTS:

2 qts. fresh blueberries
Juice of one lemon
3 cups water
¼ cup chopped fresh basil

DIRECTIONS:

1. Put all ingredients in slow cooker and stir to combine.

2. Cover and cook on low for 4 hours.

Bring a unique twist
to breakfast by
adding fresh herbs!

Macadamia Breakfast Bake and Pineapple Syrup

Macadamia Breakfast Bake

INGREDIENTS:

1 loaf French bread, sliced 1-inch thick
8 oz. can mandarin oranges, drained
8 oz. can chunk pineapple, drained,
    juice reserved
6 eggs, beaten
1 cup evaporated milk
1 cup sugar
1 Tbsp. vanilla
½ tsp. nutmeg
2 tsp. cinnamon
1 cup coconut milk
1 cup macadamia nuts, chopped
½ cup organic coconut, flaked

You know it's going to be a good day when you wake up smelling this casserole!

DIRECTIONS:

1. Place half the bread slices in greased slow cooker, covering the bottom. Place the oranges and pineapple on top of the bread. Layer the remaining bread slices on top of the fruit.

2. In large bowl, mix together reserved pineapple juice, eggs, evaporated milk, sugar, vanilla, nutmeg, cinnamon, coconut milk, macadamia nuts, and coconut. Pour mixture over bread.

3. Cover and cook on low setting for 4 hours. Serve with Pineapple Syrup.

Pineapple Syrup

INGREDIENTS:

4 cups water
½ cup brown sugar
14 oz. crushed pineapple, undrained
1 tsp. coconut extract

DIRECTIONS:

1. Add water, brown sugar, and pineapple to slow cooker. Stir to combine.

2. Cover and cook on warm for 6 to 8 hours, or overnight.

3. Stir in coconut extract just before serving. Spoon over individual portions of Macadamia Breakfast Bake.

Friendship Tea

INGREDIENTS:

    8 cups boiling water
    6 black tea bags
    2 cinnamon sticks
    8 to 10 whole cloves
    1 qt. pineapple juice
    1 qt. orange juice
    1 qt. apple juice
    1 cup lemon juice, freshly squeezed
    1 lemon
    1 orange

This rich, fruity tea will make any morning better—especially if you're sharing a mug with a friend!

DIRECTIONS:

1. Pour boiling water into slow cooker. Add tea bags, cinnamon sticks, and whole cloves. Steep 5 to 7 minutes. Remove tea bags and discard.

2. Pour pineapple juice, orange juice, apple juice, and lemon juice into slow cooker and stir to combine.

3. Cook on low overnight. In the morning, strain off and dispose of the cinnamon sticks and whole cloves. Ladle into individual mugs and garnish with thin slices of lemon and orange.

Little Piggies in a Blanket

INGREDIENTS:

1 tube refrigerated crescents
8 mini hotdogs or mini sausages
Honey Dijon mustard, to serve

DIRECTIONS:

1. Grease slow cooker well. Roll each mini sausage in a roll of crescent dough and arrange in bottom of slow cooker. Cover and cook on high for 1½ to 2 hours.

2. Serve with honey Dijon mustard for dipping.

Oh My Darling Clementines

INGREDIENTS:

12 clementines
2 cups mango juice
2 cups orange juice
2 cups apple juice
1 Tbsp. cinnamon sugar
¼ cup sliced almonds

DIRECTIONS:

1. Peel clementines but do not separate sections. Place in bottom of slow cooker.

2. Pour juices over the clementines. Cover and cook on warm overnight.

3. To serve, spoon out the clementines and place on a serving plate. Sprinkle cinnamon sugar and sliced almonds over clementines.

This is my children's favorite way to eat clementines!

Sausage, Egg, & Cheese Casserole

INGREDIENTS:

14 slices bread
1 Tbsp. honey Dijon mustard
1 dozen eggs
2¼ cups milk
2½ cups shredded cheddar cheese
1 lb. sausage, browned
1½ tsp. salt
1 tsp. pepper

DIRECTIONS:

1. Grease slow cooker thoroughly. Spread mustard on bread and cut into large squares. Place slices in slow cooker until the bottom is covered.

2. Spoon a layer of sausage over the bread, then top with cheese. Continue layering the bread, sausage, and cheese, ending with the cheese.

3. Beat the eggs well, then add milk, salt, and pepper. Pour mixture over cheese.

4. Cover and cook on low for 6 to 8 hours.

Peaches & Cream
and Heavenly Hash Browns

Peaches & Cream

INGREDIENTS:

8 fresh peaches, peeled and sliced
2 tsp. cinnamon
½ tsp. ground cloves
2 Tbsp. lemon juice
2 Tbsp. apple cider
2 Tbsp. honey
Greek yogurt

DIRECTIONS:

1. In small bowl, combine cinnamon, cloves, lemon juice, apple cider, and honey.

2. Place peach slices in slow cooker. Pour liquid over peaches. Cover and cook on low for 6 to 8 hours.

3. To serve, spoon peaches over Greek yogurt.

Heavenly Hash Browns

INGREDIENTS:

6 baking potatoes, cut into shoestrings
1 onion, chopped
1 portabella mushroom, chopped small
6 Tbsp. olive oil, divided
3 tsp. garlic salt, divided
3 tsp. freshly ground black pepper, divided

DIRECTIONS:

1. Pour 2 Tbsp. olive oil into bottom of slow cooker. Layer ⅓ of potatoes, ⅓ of onions, ⅓ of mushrooms, 1 tsp. garlic salt, and 1 tsp. pepper in slow cooker. Repeat twice for three layers of each ingredient.

2. Pour remaining olive oil over potato mixture. Cover and cook on low for 6 to 7 hours.

Make sure to serve the hash browns with a good squeeze of ketchup!

Sunrise Barley
and Fruit Compote

Sunrise Barley

INGREDIENTS:

1 cup uncooked barley
6 cups water
1 vanilla bean
½ tsp. almond extract

DIRECTIONS:

1. Combine barley and water in slow cooker. Slice vanilla bean with a sharp knife and add to pot. Cover and cook on low 6 to 8 hours.

2. Remove vanilla bean and stir in almond extract just before serving.

Sunrise Barley is a great way to greet any new day!

Fruit Compote

INGREDIENTS:

12 oz. dried apricots
2 tangerines, peeled and sectioned
12 oz. dried prunes
1 29-oz. can sliced peaches, undrained
¼ cup golden raisins
2 cups white grape juice
1 cinnamon stick

DIRECTIONS:

1. Combine all ingredients in slow cooker. Cover and cook on low for 6 to 8 hours.

2. To serve, remove cinnamon stick. Spoon over bowls of Sunrise Barley.

Chapter 2

Shopping Local, Cooking Fresh

*"I will send you the rain in its season, and the ground
will yield its crops and the trees their fruit."*

LEVITICUS 26:4

Harvest-Time Halibut Chowder and Rhubarb Crumble

Harvest-Time Halibut Chowder

INGREDIENTS:

½ cup butter
1 clove garlic, minced
1 small onion, minced
3 stalks celery, chopped
3 large carrots, chopped
1 cup flour
3 qts. water
2 qts. chicken stock, preferably homemade
4 large potatoes, unpeeled and cut in small cubes
1 lb. uncooked boneless halibut, cut into 1-inch pieces
2 tsp. salt
½ tsp. freshly ground black pepper
1 cup half-and-half or nonfat evaporated milk
4 oz. slivered almonds
6 sprigs fresh dill, chopped

Fish chowder takes the chill out of any late autumn day!

DIRECTIONS:

1. Melt butter in a large pan. Add garlic, onion, celery, and carrots. Toss until garlic becomes fragrant, about two minutes. Add flour and stir to combine for 30 seconds, taking care not to burn.

2. Add contents of pan to slow cooker. Stir in water, chicken stock, potatoes, halibut, salt, and pepper. Cover and cook on low for 6 to 8 hours, stirring occasionally.

3. Half an hour before serving, add half-and-half or evaporated milk to pot. Stir, then cover and cook an additional 30 minutes.

4. Ladle into bowls and sprinkle slivered almonds and fresh dill over each serving.

Rhubarb Crumble

INGREDIENTS:

1 cup flour
¾ cup old-fashioned rolled oats
1 cup light brown sugar, packed
1 tsp. ground cinnamon
½ cup butter, melted
4 egg whites, beaten
¾ cup sugar
½ tsp. baking soda
3 Tbsp. whole wheat flour
1 cup vanilla ice cream, softened
4 cups fresh rhubarb, finely chopped
Vanilla ice cream, to serve

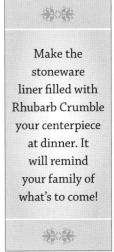

Make the stoneware liner filled with Rhubarb Crumble your centerpiece at dinner. It will remind your family of what's to come!

DIRECTIONS:

1. Grease inside of slow cooker.

2. In a small bowl, combine flour, rolled oats, brown sugar, cinnamon, and melted butter using a fork or pastry blender. Place half this mixture in bottom of slow cooker.

3. In a second bowl, beat egg whites. Add sugar, baking soda, whole wheat flour, and softened ice cream. Stir to combine, then fold in chopped rhubarb.

4. Spread the rhubarb mixture over the bottom crust. Sprinkle the remaining crumble mixture over the rhubarb.

5. Cover and cook on high for 3 to 4 hours. To serve, scoop out and top with vanilla ice cream.

Herbivore Snow Pizzatizers and Turkey Stew Solos

Herbivore Snow Pizzatizers

INGREDIENTS:

1 refrigerated tube crescent rolls
½ cup mayonnaise
2 oz. goat cheese
¼ cup parmesan cheese, grated
4 fresh green onions, chopped
2 Tbsp. fresh Italian herbs, chopped small (see note)
3 cloves garlic, minced

DIRECTIONS:

1. Grease inside of slow cooker. Line entire bottom with crescent roll dough, pressing the seams together and pushing dough 1 inch up the sides of the pot.

2. In separate bowl mix together goat cheese, mayonnaise, parmesan cheese, green onions, fresh Italian herbs, and garlic. Spread over crust.

3. Cook on low for 2 to 3 hours. To serve, cut into appetizer-size pieces.

I love a combination of basil, thyme, and oregano, but feel free to experiment with your favorite herbs!

Turkey Stew Solos

INGREDIENTS:

6 turkey patties
3 sweet potatoes, peeled and cut into shoestrings
4 carrots, cut into slices
2 oz. fresh green beans, trimmed
1 onion, sliced
1 cup chicken stock
½ cup barbecue sauce
1 tsp. salt
1 tsp. freshly ground black pepper

DIRECTIONS:

1. For each patty, place 2 9-inch pieces of foil on the counter and pinch together to make a double foil "bed."

2. Place 1 patty and ample vegetables of your choice on each bed of foil, topping with several spoonfuls of chicken stock and 1 Tbsp. barbecue sauce.

3. Add salt and pepper to taste and wrap up sides and top of foil to create a pouch. Place individual pouches in slow cooker, seam side up. Cover and cook on low setting for 4 to 6 hours.

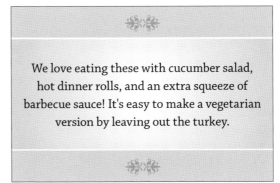

We love eating these with cucumber salad, hot dinner rolls, and an extra squeeze of barbecue sauce! It's easy to make a vegetarian version by leaving out the turkey.

French Countryside Soup and Salmon on Gingered Carrots

French Countryside Soup

INGREDIENTS:

- 4 Tbsp. butter
- 3 lbs. onions, sliced
- 1 tsp. salt
- 2 qts. best-quality beef stock, not diluted
- 2 bay leaves
- 6 sprigs fresh thyme, tied with kitchen twine
- ½ tsp. freshly ground black pepper
- 1 French baguette, cut into ½-inch slices
- 2 cups gruyère cheese, grated

DIRECTIONS:

1. Melt butter in large sauté pan. Add onions and salt and sauté over medium heat until deep golden brown, about 20 minutes. Don't worry if they begin to burn.

2. Put onions in slow cooker, scraping browned bits in as well. Add beef stock, bay leaves, thyme, and pepper.

3. Cover and cook on low for 6 to 8 hours.

4. Shortly before serving, preheat oven to 400°. Arrange baguette slices on a cookie sheet and bake until golden, about 10 minutes. Remove from oven and preheat broiler.

5. Remove bay leaves and thyme. Ladle soup into small individual ovenproof bowls. Top each with a baguette slice, toasted side down. Sprinkle gruyère evenly over bowls. Place bowls on cookie sheet and broil until cheese is melted and bubbly, 3 to 5 minutes. Let cool slightly before serving.

Salmon on Gingered Carrots

INGREDIENTS:

¼ cup olive oil
2 cloves fresh garlic, minced
4 large carrots, peeled and sliced
2 tsp. grated fresh ginger
2 lbs. salmon fillets
Salt and pepper to taste
2 sprigs fresh dill
¼ cup sliced almonds

DIRECTIONS:

1. Place olive oil, garlic, carrots, and ginger in greased slow cooker and stir to combine. Cover and cook on high for 2 hours.

2. Place fish fillets on top of carrots and sprinkle with salt, pepper, dill, and almonds.

3. Cover and cook for 1 hour or until salmon flakes when tested with a fork. (Start to test after 30 minutes of cooking.)

4. Place carrots on serving plate and top with salmon.

Slow-cooker salmon is
easy to make, healthy,
and so delicious.

Caramelized Onions and Presto Split Pea Soup

Caramelized Onions

INGREDIENTS:

3 sweet onions, sliced
¼ cup butter, melted
½ cup olive oil
½ tsp. salt
1 tsp. dried thyme
4 oz. Havarti cheese with dill, sliced
Whole grain pita chips, to serve

DIRECTIONS:

1. Combine onions, butter, olive oil, salt, and thyme in slow cooker. Cover and cook on low for 8 to 10 hours or until onions are caramelized, stirring the mixture occasionally.

2. Thirty minutes before serving, layer Havarti slices over onions. Cover and let cook 30 minutes, or until cheese is melted and bubbly.

3. Serve with whole grain pita chips.

The small of onions cooking always brings back memories of the August State Fair!

Presto Split Pea Soup

INGREDIENTS:

1 lb. dry split peas, washed and sorted
2 tsp. garlic powder
1 Tbsp. olive oil
2 qts. plus 2 cups water
2 bay leaves
1 stalk celery, chopped small
2 large carrots, peeled and chopped small
Salt and pepper, to taste
1 cup evaporated milk
⅓ lb. fully-cooked turkey ham, cubed

DIRECTIONS:

1. Add the split peas, garlic powder, olive oil, water, bay leaves, celery, carrots, salt, and pepper to slow cooker. Stir to combine.

2. Cover and cook on low for 8 to 10 hours.

3. Twenty minutes before serving, remove bay leaves and stir in evaporated milk and ham. Allow to heat up before serving.

Salsa Chicken
and Smooth Strawberry Sorbet

Salsa Chicken

INGREDIENTS:

- 2 lbs. boneless, skinless chicken breasts, cut into 1-inch wide strips
- 1 Tbsp. chili powder
- ¼ tsp. garlic powder
- ¼ tsp. crushed red pepper flakes
- ¼ tsp. dried oregano
- ½ tsp. paprika
- 1½ tsp. ground cumin
- 1 tsp. freshly ground black pepper
- 2 Tbsp. flour
- 1 green bell pepper, seeded and cut into 1-inch wide strips
- 1 red bell pepper, seeded and cut into 1-inch wide strips
- 1 cup corn
- 1 16-oz. jar best-quality salsa, divided
- 2 cups brown rice, cooked

DIRECTIONS:

1. Grease inside of slow cooker. In a separate bowl, combine spices and flour. Coat each chicken strip in spice mixture.

2. Pour half of salsa in bottom of slow cooker and place coated chicken strips on top of salsa. Layer peppers and corn on top of chicken, and top with remaining salsa.

3. Cover and cook on low for 6 to 8 hours. Spoon over cooked brown rice to serve.

Smooth Strawberry Sorbet

INGREDIENTS:

  2 qts. fresh strawberries, hulled
  ½ cup frozen orange juice concentrate
  1 Tbsp. fresh lemon juice
  1 Tbsp. fresh lime juice

DIRECTIONS:

1. Puree all ingredients in a food processor and pour into a slow cooker stoneware liner.

2. Cover and freeze for at least 4 hours. For a smooth consistency, remove from freezer and stir the puree every 60 minutes for the first 2 hours.

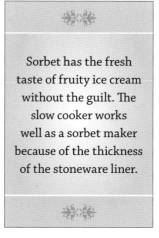

Sorbet has the fresh taste of fruity ice cream without the guilt. The slow cooker works well as a sorbet maker because of the thickness of the stoneware liner.

Lemon-Dill Scallops and Pineapple Carrots

Lemon-Dill Scallops

INGREDIENTS:

2 lbs. scallops
½ cup ranch dressing
¼ cup fresh dill, chopped very small
¼ cup lemon juice, freshly squeezed
¼ tsp. white pepper

DIRECTIONS:

1. Grease inside of slow cooker and place scallops in the bottom. Pour dressing over scallops and sprinkle with fresh dill.

2. Cover and cook on low for 2 hours. Squeeze fresh lemon juice and white pepper over top to serve.

This exquisite combination of lemon and dill is destined to become a family favorite!

Pineapple Carrots

INGREDIENTS:

- 2 lbs. carrots, peeled and sliced
- 2 cups pineapple chunks
- 2 Tbsp. butter, melted
- 2 tsp. salt
- 1 tsp. vanilla
- 1 cup orange juice
- 2 Tbsp. brown sugar
- 2 Tbsp. fresh parsley, chopped

DIRECTIONS:

1. Put carrots, pineapple, melted butter, salt, vanilla, and orange juice in greased slow cooker. Stir to combine and sprinkle with brown sugar.

2. Cover and cook on low for 3 to 5 hours. To serve, sprinkle with chopped parsley.

Pomegranate-Raspberry Punch

INGREDIENTS:

- 1 32-oz. bottle pomegranate juice, chilled until ice crystals begin to form
- 1 2-liter bottle raspberry ginger ale, chilled until ice crystals begin to form
- 1 pint fresh raspberries

DIRECTIONS:

1. Mix the juice and fresh raspberries in a freezer-chilled slow cooker stoneware liner.

2. Stir in the raspberry ginger ale and ladle into small glasses.

This punch adds a touch of elegance to any ordinary dinner!

Farmer's Market Stew

INGREDIENTS:

- 1 lb. ground sausage
- 1 onion, chopped
- 2 cloves garlic, minced
- 3 red bliss potatoes, quartered
- 3 large carrots, sliced
- 1 stalk celery, chopped
- 1 cup green peas
- 1 cup corn
- 3 large tomatoes, chopped
- 1 tsp. salt
- ½ tsp. pepper
- 1 tsp. cumin
- 2 bay leaves
- 2 qts. plus 2 cups chicken broth, preferably homemade

DIRECTIONS:

There are endless variations on this soup. We like it with cheese sprinkled on top, or with some cooked noodles added at the end of cooking. Use your imagination! I also like to change this up by seeing what local produce is available at the farmer's market.

1. Brown ground sausage in sauté pan on stovetop. Drain and transfer sausage to slow cooker. Place onions in empty pan and cook over medium heat until softened, 5-8 minutes. Add onions to slow cooker with all remaining ingredients. Stir to combine.

2. Cover and cook on low for 7 to 8 hours. To serve, remove bay leaves.

Baked Potatoes
and Broccoli-Cheese Topping

Baked Potatoes

INGREDIENTS:

8 baking potatoes, scrubbed
8 tsp. olive oil, divided
¼ cup kosher salt
Aluminum foil for wrapping potatoes

DIRECTIONS:

1. Lay out a square of aluminum foil for each potato. Rub each potato with 1 tsp. olive oil and 1½ tsp. kosher salt. Wrap foil up and around until potato is completely covered. Stick each potato several times with a fork.

2. Fill dry slow cooker with the wrapped potatoes. Cover and cook on high for 2 to 3 hours (or until potatoes are tender when poked with a fork).

This is one of our favorite comfort-food meals!

Broccoli-Cheese Topping

INGREDIENTS:

½ cup sharp cheddar cheese, grated
½ cup parmesan cheese, grated
1 cup mozzarella cheese, shredded
1 cup swiss cheese, grated
1 small onion, minced
½ cup mayonnaise
3 cups broccoli, chopped fine
pinch cayenne pepper (optional)

DIRECTIONS:

1. Combine all ingredients in slow cooker. Cover and cook on low for 2 to 3 hours.

2. To serve, spoon over halved Baked Potatoes.

For an extra treat, crumble bacon over the potatoes!

Wisconsin Cranberry Stuffing and Buttermilk Chicken

Wisconsin Cranberry Stuffing

INGREDIENTS:

6 Tbsp. butter, divided
4 cups cubed whole wheat bread
2 tsp. thyme
2 tsp. rosemary
2 tsp. sage
2 tsp. oregano
1 tsp. freshly ground black pepper
2 stalks celery, chopped
1 small onion, chopped
2 cups chicken stock, preferably homemade
1 cup fresh cranberries, chopped
1 apple, peeled and chopped
½ cup golden raisins
1 cup walnuts, chopped

DIRECTIONS:

1. Preheat oven to 350°. In large bowl, combine bread and spices. Melt ¼ cup butter and pour over bread. Toss to combine. Spread bread cubes on large rimmed baking sheet in single layer. Bake until golden, 15 to 20 minutes. Transfer to slow cooker.

2. In the meantime, heat remaining 2 Tbsp. butter in sauté pan over medium heat. Add the celery and onion. Cook, stirring occasionally, until softened, about 5 minutes. Transfer to slow cooker.

3. Combine all remaining ingredients in slow cooker and toss to combine. Cover and cook on low for 4 to 6 hours.

Buttermilk Chicken

INGREDIENTS:

2 lbs. boneless, skinless chicken breasts
2 cups buttermilk
3 Tbsp. chopped fresh rosemary
1 tsp. salt
2 Tbsp olive oil
1 Tbsp. freshly ground black pepper

DIRECTIONS:

1. Combine chicken, buttermilk, rosemary, and salt in large freezer bag. Place in refrigerator and marinate 12 to 24 hours.

2. Drain off marinade and place chicken in bottom of slow cooker. Drizzle olive oil over chicken and sprinkle with pepper.

3. Cover and cook on low for 6 hours.

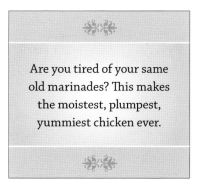

Are you tired of your same old marinades? This makes the moistest, plumpest, yummiest chicken ever.

Tropical Orange Roughy
and Spicy Brussels Sprouts

Tropical Orange Roughy

INGREDIENTS:

- 2 oranges, peeled and cut into sections
- ½ cup shredded coconut
- ½ cup pineapple chunks
- 1 mango, sliced
- ½ cup low-fat Greek yogurt
- 2 lbs. Orange Roughy fillets
- 2 Tbsp. fresh chives, chopped
- 2 tsp. fresh basil, chopped fine
- 2 cups brown rice, cooked

DIRECTIONS:

1. Place fish fillets in bottom of greased slow cooker.

2. In a separate bowl, combine oranges, coconut, pineapple, mango, and yogurt. Spread mixture over fish and sprinkle with chives and basil.

3. Cover and cook on low for 1 hour. Don't overcook.

4. Serve fish over cooked brown rice.

Spicy Brussels Sprouts

INGREDIENTS:

32 oz. Brussels sprouts
¼ cup olive oil
¼ cup water
1 tsp. freshly ground black pepper
½ cup pine nuts
½ cup sliced almonds
½ tsp. paprika

DIRECTIONS:

1. Combine Brussels sprouts, olive oil, and pepper in slow cooker. Mix well. Cover and cook on low for 3 hours.

2. To serve, toss Brussels sprouts with pine nuts and almonds and sprinkle with paprika.

Even my children like Brussels sprouts prepared this way!

Pizzzza Dip

INGREDIENTS:

¼ cup olive oil
1 medium onion, minced
2 cloves garlic, minced
6 Roma tomatoes, diced
8 oz. button mushrooms, sliced thin
1 green bell pepper, seeded and chopped
2 6-oz. cans tomato paste
1 32-oz. can tomato sauce
1 tsp. salt
1 Tbsp. dried oregano
2 tsp. dried basil
1 tsp. dried thyme
4 oz. Parmesan cheese, freshly grated, to serve
Whole grain pita chips, to serve

These will be the most popular dips at any gathering!

DIRECTIONS:

1. Combine all ingredients except parmesan and pita chips in slow cooker. Mix well. Cover and cook on low for 6 hours.

2. Preheat oven to 350°. Arrange pita chips on rimmed baking sheet in single layer. Sprinkle grated parmesan over chips and bake until golden, 10 to 15 minutes.

3. Serve dip with parmesan chips and a fresh-cut veggie tray.

Sombrero Party Dip

INGREDIENTS:

1½ lbs. ground turkey
1 Tbsp. olive oil
2 cloves garlic, minced
1 tsp. chili powder
½ tsp. paprika
½ tsp. ground cumin
½ tsp. ground dried chipotle chili pepper
2 cups diced tomatoes
1 avocado, peeled and chopped
1 16-oz. can black beans, drained
1 red pepper, seeded and chopped
1 green pepper, seeded and chopped
1 bunch green onions, chopped
2 15-oz. cans refried beans
1 12-oz. jar of chunky salsa
2 cups shredded cheddar cheese
1 8-oz. can black olives, drained and sliced
1 cup low-fat sour cream

DIRECTIONS:

1. In a sauté pan over medium heat, lightly brown turkey with olive oil, garlic, and spices.

2. Transfer half of turkey to the bottom of the slow cooker. Layer the tomatoes, avocado, black beans, peppers, green onions, refried beans, and salsa. Add remaining half of turkey. Cover and cook on low for 4 hours.

3. Add cheese and black olives. Cover and cook on low 1 additional hour.

4. Serve with a fresh-cut veggie tray and sour cream on the side.

Oklahoma Brisket
and Twin Zucchini Casserole

Oklahoma Brisket

INGREDIENTS:

4 sweet potatoes, peeled and sliced
1 5-lb. beef brisket
2 Tbsp. lemon juice
2 Tbsp. Worcestershire sauce
2 tsp. salt
2 tsp. seasoning salt
2 tsp. freshly ground pepper
2 Tbsp. beef base or bouillon granules
2 Tbsp. instant coffee crystals
2 tsp. white vinegar
2 tsp. honey
4 cloves garlic, minced
1 small onion, chopped
2 cups water

DIRECTIONS:

1. Scatter sweet potato slices around bottom of greased pot. Set brisket (cut in half to fit, if necessary) on top of potatoes.

2. Mix all remaining ingredients in separate bowl and pour over brisket. Cover and cook on low for 8 to 10 hours.

3. Carve brisket and serve with sweet potatoes and sauce spooned over.

Twin Zucchini Casserole

INGREDIENTS:

1¾ cup flour
2 tsp. baking powder
¼ tsp. salt
⅓ cup vegetable shortening
¼ cup extra virgin olive oil
2 egg whites, beaten
½ cup milk
2 tsp. fresh basil, chopped fine
2 tsp. freshly ground black pepper
2 tsp. chives, chopped fine
2 cups green zucchini, sliced thin
2 cups yellow zucchini, sliced thin
¾ cup parmesan cheese, grated fresh

DIRECTIONS:

1. In a medium bowl, use pastry blender to combine flour, baking powder, salt, and shortening. Create well in center and add olive oil, egg whites, milk, basil, pepper, and chives. Stir to combine.

2. Transfer mixture to slow cooker and press into all sides. Layer zucchini slices over crust, then sprinkle parmesan cheese over zucchini.

3. Cover and cook on low for 3 to 4 hours. (Place a fork between the slow cooker and the lid to ventilate for the last hour.)

Chapter 3

Passport to the Nations

*Be still, and know that I am God; I will be exalted
among the nations, I will be exalted in the earth.*

PSALM 46:10

Frijoles Charros

INGREDIENTS:

1 onion, chopped
½ lb. ground sausage
6 slices bacon, crumbled
3 15.5-oz. cans pinto beans, rinsed and drained
1 cup water
1 28-oz. can diced tomatoes
4 Serrano chilies, minced (optional)
1 Tbsp. cumin
1 tsp. salt
1 tsp. freshly ground black pepper

DIRECTIONS:

1. Brown sausage and onion in large sauté pan over medium heat. Transfer to greased slow cooker and add all remaining ingredients. Stir to combine.

2. Cover and cook on low for 6 to 8 hours.

You won't need an interpreter to figure out the message of this dish—"Delicious!"

Stuffed Peppers

INGREDIENTS:

6 green bell peppers
1 large onion, chopped
2 cloves garlic, minced
1 6-oz. can tomato paste
2 Roma tomatoes, diced
3 cups cooked couscous
⅓ cup canned black beans, rinsed and drained
½ tsp. cumin
½ tsp. salt
½ tsp. freshly ground black pepper
½ cup water

DIRECTIONS:

1. Cut off tops of peppers and remove seeds. Set peppers upright in slow cooker.

2. Combine onion, garlic, tomato paste, tomatoes, couscous, black beans, cumin, salt, and pepper in separate bowl and mix well. Spoon stuffing into peppers.

3. Pour water in slow cooker around the peppers. Cover and cook on low for 6 to 8 hours, or until peppers are tender.

Easy Cabbage Rolls

INGREDIENTS:

1 cabbage head
4 cups water
1 lb. ground turkey
¼ cup onion, grated
½ cup rice, uncooked
1 tsp. freshly ground black pepper
1 tsp. salt
1 tsp. dried thyme
1 tsp. dried nutmeg
1 tsp. cinnamon
1 can tomato soup
5 cups water

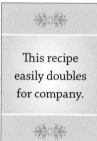

This recipe easily doubles for company.

DIRECTIONS:

1. Rinse cabbage leaves and place in large, heatproof bowl. Boil 4 cups water and pour over cabbage leaves. Soak leaves for 5 minutes, then drain water and let leaves cool.

2. Brown turkey and onion in large sauté pan over medium heat. Remove from heat and stir in rice, pepper, salt, thyme, nutmeg, and cinnamon.

3. Place 3 Tbsp. meat and rice mixture on each cabbage leaf and roll up tightly. Stack rolls in greased slow cooker.

4. Combine tomato soup and water in separate bowl. Pour over stuffed cabbage. Cover and cook on low for 6 hours.

Mediterranean Rice Pilaf

INGREDIENTS:

2 Tbsp. olive oil
1 small onion, chopped
2 cups long grain brown rice
3 cups water
2 cups chicken stock
1½ tsp. salt
¼ cup chopped dried apricots
¼ cup golden raisins
¼ cup toasted pine nuts
¼ cup chopped fresh parsley
1 tsp. cinnamon

DIRECTIONS:

1. Combine olive oil, onions, rice, water, chicken stock, salt, apricots, and raisins in slow cooker. Cover and cook on low for 2 to 3 hours, or until rice is cooked. Place a fork between the slow cooker and lid for ventilation.

2. Uncover and fluff the rice gently with a fork. Stir in pine nuts and transfer to serving dish. Sprinkle cinnamon and parsley on top.

African Sweet Potatoes and Kikuyu Chicken

African Sweet Potatoes

INGREDIENTS:

6 sweet potatoes, peeled and cut into ½-inch slices
4 Tbsp. butter, melted
1 tsp. cinnamon
1 tsp. cumin
1 tsp. turmeric
1 tsp. curry powder

DIRECTIONS:

1. Combine cinnamon, cumin, turmeric, and curry powder in small bowl. Set aside.

2. Put sweet potato slices in bottom of slow cooker. Drizzle melted butter over slices, then sprinkle spice mixture over top. Toss with rubber spatula to combine.

3. Cover and cook on low for 4 to 6 hours, or until potatoes are tender.

Kikuyu Chicken

INGREDIENTS:

2 lbs. chicken thighs
1 14.5-oz. can stewed tomatoes
1 onion, chopped
1 Tbsp. turmeric
1 Tbsp. garlic powder
½ tsp. chili powder
½ tsp. curry powder
2 Tbsp. tomato paste
1 tsp. salt
1 tsp. freshly ground pepper
Cooked long grain brown rice, to serve

DIRECTIONS:

1. Put tomatoes, onion, turmeric, garlic powder, chili powder, curry powder, tomato paste, salt, and pepper in slow cooker. Stir to combine. Add chicken thighs and spoon tomato mixture over top.

2. Cover and cook on low for 4 to 6 hours. Serve over cooked rice.

All-American Pulled Beef and Molasses Baked Beans

All-American Pulled Beef

INGREDIENTS:

1 4-lb. rump roast
2 12-oz cans root beer
½ cup onion, grated
1½ cups ketchup
½ cup molasses
¼ cup cider vinegar
¼ cup Worcestershire sauce
¼ cup Dijon mustard
1 tsp. hot pepper sauce
¼ tsp. freshly ground black pepper
2 cloves garlic, minced
1 tsp. chili powder
¼ tsp. cayenne pepper
8 hamburger buns (to serve)
2 cups coleslaw (to serve)

As American as apple pie! Our kids are barbecue connoisseurs, and they rate this pulled beef at the top.

DIRECTIONS:

1. In medium bowl, mix together onion, ketchup, molasses, cider vinegar, Worcestershire sauce, mustard, hot pepper sauce, pepper, garlic, chili powder, and cayenne. Remove 1½ cups of sauce and set aside. Pour root beer into bowl and whisk to combine.

2. Put rump roast in slow cooker. Pour root beer mixture over tenderloin, then cover and cook on low to 5 to 7 hours.

3. Drain off liquid and shred the beef using two forks. Mix in reserved sauce. Cover and cook 1 to 2 hours.

4. To serve, spoon onto buns and top with coleslaw.

Molasses Baked Beans

INGREDIENTS:

1 lb. dry navy beans
8 cups water
1 cup brown sugar, packed
1 Tbsp. dry mustard
¼ cup molasses
1 tsp. salt
¼ tsp. ground cloves
1 onion, minced
4 strips bacon, chopped fine

DIRECTIONS:

1. Combine the beans and water in a large saucepan. Bring to a boil and cook for 1½ hours. Pour beans and liquid into a bowl, cover, and refrigerate overnight.

2. Drain off liquid, reserving one cup. Pour beans and reserved liquid into slow cooker and stir in remaining ingredients. Cover and cook on low for 8 to 10 hours.

Peanut Wings

INGREDIENTS:

1 cup orange juice
1 cup chicken broth
¼ cup low sodium soy sauce
¼ cup brown sugar
1 tsp. ground ginger
⅛ tsp. freshly ground black pepper
¼ tsp. garlic powder
3 lbs. chicken wings
½ cup peanut butter
¼ cup crushed peanuts,
    for garnish
Brown rice, to serve

This is a great—
and not too spicy—
variation on the
typical barbecue and
hot wing recipes.

DIRECTIONS:

1. Combine orange juice, chicken broth, soy sauce, brown sugar, ginger, pepper, and garlic in slow cooker. Mix well, then add chicken wings. Stir to coat. Cover and cook on low for 3 hours.

2. Add peanut butter and stir to combine. Cover and cook on low for 1 additional hour.

3. Sprinkle with crushed peanuts and serve over brown rice.

Asian Scallop "Stir Fry"

INGREDIENTS:

 2 cups chicken broth
 3 carrots, peeled and sliced
 1 red bell pepper, seeded and chopped
 2 cloves garlic, minced
 1 Tbsp. fresh ginger, grated
 1 8-oz. can water chestnuts
 2 8-oz. packages bean sprouts
 1 lb. scallops
 2 tsp. sesame oil

DIRECTIONS:

1. Combine the broth, carrots, pepper, garlic, ginger, water chestnuts, and bean sprouts in the slow cooker. Cover and cook on low for 2 to 4 hours.

2. Add the scallops and sesame oil. Stir to coat. Cover and cook on low about 30 minutes, or until scallops are done.

Saag Aloo
and Coconut Chicken Curry

Saag Aloo

INGREDIENTS:

2 Tbsp. olive oil
2 Tbsp. butter, melted
1 large onion, chopped
2 large baking potatoes, cubed
1 quart water
1 tsp. fresh ginger, grated
1 clove garlic, chopped
½ tsp. cumin
1 Tbsp. turmeric
1 tsp. garam masala
1 tsp. salt
1 lb. fresh spinach, chopped
Basmati rice, to serve

Your family will love the unique flavors in these Indian dishes.

DIRECTIONS:

1. Combine olive oil, butter, onion, potatoes, water, ginger, garlic, cumin, turmeric, garam masala, and salt in slow cooker. Mix well. Cover and cook on low for 3 hours.

2. Add the spinach and stir to combine. Cook on low for 1 additional hour. Serve over basmati rice.

Coconut Chicken Curry

INGREDIENTS:

1 Tbsp. olive oil
3 lbs. boneless, skinless chicken breasts, cut into strips
1 medium onion, sliced
1 14-oz. can coconut milk
2 tsp. salt
1 tsp. freshly ground black pepper
3 Tbsp. curry powder
2 tsp. hot pepper sauce
1 cup chicken broth, preferably homemade
8 oz. sugar snap peas
2 to 3 Tbsp. toasted flaked coconut

DIRECTIONS:

1. Heat olive oil in large skillet until shimmering. Add chicken strips and heat until cooked through and beginning to brown, 8 to 10 minutes.

2. Add the sliced onion to the slow cooker and layer the cooked chicken on top.

3. In a separate bowl, mix coconut milk, salt, pepper, curry, hot pepper sauce, and broth. Whisk to combine. Pour coconut milk mixture over chicken. Cover and cook on low 4 to 6 hours.

4. Add the peas, stirring to combine. Cover and cook on low 1 additional hour. Sprinkle with coconut to serve.

Ribolitta Soup and Basil Dipping Oil

Ribollita Soup

INGREDIENTS

8 cloves garlic, minced
1 large onion, chopped
6 Tbsp. olive oil, divided, plus additional for serving
1 gallon water
1¼ cups dried cannellini beans, picked over and rinsed
1 Tbsp. salt
12 fresh sage leaves
2 stalks celery, diced
1 carrot, peeled and chopped
1 large unpeeled baking potato, cut into ½-inch cubes
2 tsp. dried thyme
⅓ lb. black kale, cut into 1-inch ribbons
⅓ lb. green chard, cut into 1-inch ribbons
4 cups savoy cabbage, thinly sliced
5 large plum tomatoes, chopped
1 cup freshly grated parmesan cheese
¼ tsp. dried crushed red pepper
5 cups vegetable stock
1 loaf Italian bread, cut into ½-inch slices
1 tsp. freshly ground black pepper
3 Tbsp. olive oil

DIRECTIONS:

1. Combine all ingredients except Italian bread, pepper, and olive oil in the slow cooker. Cover and cook on low for 7 to 8 hours.

2. Add Italian bread to soup and simmer 30 minutes to 1 hour, stirring often to break up bread into smaller pieces.

3. Season with pepper and divide soup among bowls. Drizzle with olive oil and serve.

Basil Dipping Oil

INGREDIENTS:

4 cups extra virgin olive oil
½ cup fresh basil leaves, chopped

DIRECTIONS:

1. Combine the olive oil and basil in slow cooker. Cover and cook on low for 3 hours.

2. Allow oil to cool for 20 minutes, and then pour it through a fine-mesh strainer into a bowl. Discard solids.

3. When oil has cooled completely, transfer to glass container, cover, and refrigerate for up to 4 weeks.

4. Drizzle onto plate and serve with sliced Italian bread.

I like to keep some of this oil on hand and serve it with crusty bread whenever I'm making an Italian meal. It also makes a delicious appetizer!

Curry Tofu and Spiced Rice

Curry Tofu

INGREDIENTS:

2 lbs. extra-firm tofu
¼ cup vegetable oil
1 red bell pepper, seeded and chopped
8 oz. sugar snap peas
2 Tbsp. fresh ginger, grated
¼ cup curry powder
6 Tbsp. lime juice, freshly squeezed
2 Tbsp. soy sauce
2 Tbsp. fish sauce
2 Tbsp. real maple syrup
2 14-oz. cans coconut milk
½ cup chopped fresh basil

This meatless meal is rich in protein and savory scents.

DIRECTIONS:

1. Heat the oil in a large skillet over medium heat until shimmering. Add the tofu and fry until golden brown.

2. Combine ginger, curry, lime juice, soy sauce, fish sauce, maple syrup, and coconut milk in slow cooker. Add tofu, pepper, and peas. Stir gently to coat. Cook on low 2 to 3 hours. Sprinkle with basil and serve over Spiced Rice.

Spiced Rice

INGREDIENTS:

- 3 cups basmati rice
- 1 Tbsp. butter
- 4 cups water
- 1 14-oz. can coconut milk
- ½ tsp. salt
- 1 cinnamon stick
- ½ tsp. nutmeg
- 1 Tbsp. whole cardamom pods

DIRECTIONS:

1. Grease slow cooker with butter. Combine all remaining ingredients in slow cooker.

2. Cover, placing a fork between the pot and the lid, and cook on high 2 to 3 hours. Remove cinnamon stick before serving.

Chicken Pitas and Greek Green Beans in Tomato Sauce

Chicken Pitas

INGREDIENTS:

2 lbs. boneless, skinless chicken breasts
1 onion, minced
¼ cup lemon juice
½ cup chicken broth
3 tsp. salt, divided
1 cup Greek yogurt
1 tsp. freshly ground black pepper
¼ tsp. cayenne pepper
1 clove garlic, minced
1 tsp. dried oregano
1 large cucumber, diced
2 tomatoes, sliced
Whole grain pita bread
½ lb. feta cheese

DIRECTIONS:

1. Combine onion, lemon juice, chicken broth, and 2 tsp. salt in slow cooker. Add chicken. Cover and cook on low 5 to 7 hours.

2. Remove chicken from slow cooker and shred with two forks. Set aside.

3. In separate bowl, combine yogurt, pepper, cayenne, 1 tsp. salt, garlic, oregano, and diced cucumber.

4. Fill pitas with shredded chicken and tomato. Top with yogurt sauce and crumbled feta cheese.

Greek Green Beans in Tomato Sauce

INGREDIENTS:

2 lbs. fresh green beans, trimmed
¼ cup lemon juice, freshly squeezed
1 medium onion, chopped
¾ cup olive oil
1 cup water
1 28-oz. can diced tomatoes
2 Tbsp. fresh parsley, chopped
2 Tbsp. fresh oregano, chopped
1 tsp. salt
1 tsp. freshly ground pepper
1 bay leaf

DIRECTIONS:

1. Combine lemon juice, onion, olive oil, water, tomatoes, parsley, oregano, salt, pepper, and bay leaf in slow cooker. Add green beans and stir to coat.

2. Cover and cook on low for 4 hours. Remove bay leaf before serving.

This Mediterranean dish is guaranteed to get your kids eating their greens!

Cuban Turkey
and Black Beans

Cuban Turkey

INGREDIENTS:

1 5-lb. turkey breast
6 fresh garlic cloves, peeled
1 onion, quartered
1 Tbsp. salt
1 Tbsp. cumin
1 Tbsp. freshly ground black pepper
1 Tbsp. dried oregano
⅓ cup fresh lime juice, freshly squeezed
⅓ cup fresh orange juice, freshly squeezed
1 onion, quartered

DIRECTIONS:

1. Combine salt, cumin, pepper, and oregano in small bowl. Set aside.

2. Grease slow cooker and set turkey breast inside. Scatter onion quarters and garlic cloves around turkey and pour lime and orange juice over top.

3. Rub spices all over turkey. Cover and cook on high 1 hour, then 5 to 7 hours on low.

Black Beans

INGREDIENTS:

1 Tbsp. olive oil
2 medium onions, chopped
8 cloves garlic, minced
1 Tbsp. cumin
1 tsp. freshly ground black pepper
1 tsp. oregano
2 tsp. salt
½ tsp. cayenne
1 red bell pepper, seeded and chopped
2 15-oz. cans black beans, drained and rinsed
½ cup water
1½ cups corn
2 Tbsp. chopped fresh cilantro (optional)

DIRECTIONS:

1. Combine olive oil, onions, garlic, cumin, pepper, oregano, salt, cayenne, bell pepper, beans, and water in slow cooker and mix well. Cover and cook on low for 4 to 6 hours. Stir in corn during last hour of cooking.

2. To serve, scatter with chopped cilantro.

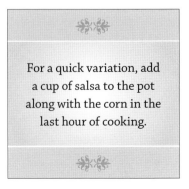

For a quick variation, add a cup of salsa to the pot along with the corn in the last hour of cooking.

Coq au Vin and French Onion Pie

Coq au Vin

INGREDIENTS:

5 slices uncooked bacon, diced
4 lbs. chicken thighs
6 small white pearl onions, peeled
½ lb. cremini or baby portabella mushrooms
4 cloves garlic, minced
1 tsp. salt
¼ tsp. freshly ground black pepper
1 tsp. fresh thyme leaves
1 bay leaf
½ cup chicken stock, preferably homemade
2 cups sparkling grape juice

DIRECTIONS:

1. Cook bacon in a large skillet until crisp. Transfer bacon to slow cooker but do not clean skillet.

2. Add chicken to skillet and cook until golden on both sides. Transfer chicken to slow cooker.

3. Add all remaining ingredients to slow cooker. Cover and cook on low for 8 hours.

Bacon adds a fresh touch to this traditional French dish.

French Onion Pie

INGREDIENTS:

1 refrigerated roll-out pie crust
½ cup olive oil
3 Tbsp. flour
3 egg whites, beaten
½ tsp. freshly ground black pepper
2 Tbsp. Worcestershire sauce
1 tsp. kosher salt
2½ lbs. Vidalia or Bermuda onions, thinly sliced
¾ cup crème fraiche
1 Tbsp. parmesan, freshly grated

DIRECTIONS:

1. Grease the inside of the slow cooker and place the crust in the bottom. Press it down and 1 inch up all sides.

2. In separate bowl, combine olive oil, flour, egg whites, pepper, Worcestershire sauce, and salt. Toss onions in this mixture and layer on top of crust in slow cooker.

3. Cover and cook on high for 4 to 6 hours.

4. To serve, top with dollops of crème fraiche and sprinkle with parmesan.

Swedish Meatballs with Gravy and Savory Mashed Potatoes

Swedish Meatballs

INGREDIENTS:

1 cup milk
1 cup cubed bread
1½ lbs. ground pork
¼ cup grated onion
2 egg whites, beaten

1 Tbsp. fresh parsley, finely chopped
1½ tsp. salt
½ tsp. freshly ground pepper
½ tsp. ginger

DIRECTIONS:

1. Preheat oven to 350°. Prepare large baking sheet by lining it with parchment paper.

2. In small bowl, soak bread in milk for 5 minutes. Mash with fork to form panade.

This is my great-grandmother's Swedish meatball recipe. I hope your family enjoys it as much as mine!

3. Transfer panade to larger bowl. Add pork, onion, egg whites, parsley, salt, pepper, and ginger. Mix with hands until nearly homogeneous.

4. Form mixture into 1-inch balls. (This process will be easier if you wet your hands between meatballs.) Place meatballs on prepared baking sheet and cook 18 to 20 minutes, until browned. Let cool five minutes and place in slow cooker.

Gravy

INGREDIENTS:

4 Tbsp. butter
2 Tbsp. flour
1 Tbsp. packed brown sugar

2½ cups chicken broth
1 cup half-and-half
1 Tbsp. lemon juice

DIRECTIONS:

1. Melt butter in saucepan. Stir in flour and cook for 1 minute until golden. Add brown sugar and stir 30 seconds until combined.

2. Add chicken broth, half-and-half, and lemon juice. Bring to a boil, then reduce heat and let simmer 10 to 15 minutes, stirring occasionally.

3. Pour the gravy over meatballs in slow cooker. Cook on low for 1 hour.

Savory Mashed Potatoes

INGREDIENTS:

5 lbs. red potatoes, quartered
1 gallon water (approx.)
4 tsp. salt, divided
6 Tbsp. butter
½ cup chicken stock
2½ cups milk
1 Tbsp. freshly ground black pepper

DIRECTIONS:

1. Put potatoes in slow cooker and add enough water to cover by 1 inch. Add 2 tsp. salt. Cover and cook on high for 4 hours. Test with a fork to see if the potatoes are done. Drain, leaving potatoes in slow cooker.

2. Add remaining 2 tsp. salt, butter, chicken stock, milk, and pepper to potatoes. Mash by hand or with electric mixer until homogeneous. Serve with Swedish meatballs and gravy.

Chapter 4

For the Kitchen with the Revolving Door

*You will eat the fruit of your labor; blessings and
prosperity will be yours. Your wife will be like a
fruitful vine within your house; your children
will be like olive shoots around your table.*

Psalm 128:2-3

Down-Home Beans

INGREDIENTS:

1 lb. dry navy beans
8 cups water
1 cup brown sugar, packed
1 Tbsp. Dijon mustard
¼ cup molasses
1 tsp. salt
¼ tsp. ground cloves
1 med. onion, minced
4 strips bacon, chopped fine

DIRECTIONS:

1. Combine the beans and water in a large saucepan. Bring to a boil and cook for 1½ hours. Pour beans and liquid into a bowl, cover, and refrigerate overnight.

2. Drain off liquid, reserving one cup. Pour beans and reserved liquid into slow cooker and stir in remaining ingredients. Cover and cook on low for 8 to 10 hours.

Corn, Corn on the Ranch

INGREDIENTS:

12 ears of corn, husk and silk removed
1 cup ranch dressing
Aluminum foil

DIRECTIONS:

1. Boil 2 qt. water in large pot. Blanch corn in water for 4 minutes, then remove and let cool slightly.

2. Tear off 12 squares of aluminum foil and stack on counter.

3. Pour ranch dressing into a plate. Roll each ear of corn in the dressing, then wrap securely in foil. Stack ears in slow cooker. Cover and cook 2 to 3 hours on low.

This is a great recipe to make corn on the cob exciting again!

Sweet 'Taters
and Ribilicious Ribs

Sweet 'Taters

INGREDIENTS:

6 sweet potatoes, peeled and sliced into ½-inch rounds
1 cup applesauce, unsweetened
2 tsp. ground cinnamon
¼ ground ginger
⅛ tsp. ground nutmeg

DIRECTIONS:

1. Place sweet potatoes in slow cooker with enough water to cover. Cover and cook 3 hours or until tender but firm.

2. Drain sweet potatoes and place in separate bowl.

3. Mash sweet potatoes with applesauce, cinnamon, ginger, and nutmeg. Return to slow cooker and top with Sweet 'Taters Topping.

Sweet 'Taters Topping

INGREDIENTS:

½ cup whole wheat flour
¼ cup butter, melted
½ cup chopped pecans
2 Tbsp. honey
2 Tbsp. brown sugar
2 large apples, peeled, cored, and cut into ¼-inch rings

DIRECTIONS:

1. Mix flour, butter, pecans, honey, and brown sugar in medium bowl. Add apple rings and toss to combine.

2. Layer topping over sweet potatoes in slow cooker. Cover and cook on low 2 to 3 hours.

Ribilicious Ribs

INGREDIENTS:

4 lbs. pork ribs
1 tsp. garlic salt
1 tsp. freshly ground black pepper
1 tsp. chili powder
1 tsp. cumin
½ tsp. dry mustard
1 Tbsp. brown sugar
1 cup barbecue sauce
½ cup ketchup
¼ cup Worcestershire sauce
¼ cup soy sauce
¼ cup orange juice
¼ cup lemon juice

These delicious ribs will have everyone in your family smacking their lips!

DIRECTIONS:

1. Combine garlic salt, pepper, chili powder, cumin, dry mustard, and brown sugar in small bowl. Massage spice rub into ribs. Place ribs in bottom of slow cooker.

2. In separate bowl, combine barbecue sauce, ketchup, Worcestershire sauce, soy sauce, orange juice, and lemon juice. Pour sauce over ribs.

3. Cover and cook on low 7 to 8 hours, or until ribs are tender.

Chicago Italian Chicken & Brats and Cinque Beans

Chicago Italian Chicken & Brats

INGREDIENTS:

2 lbs. boneless, skinless chicken breasts
¾ cup white vinegar
1 cup olive oil
2 cloves garlic, minced
2 tsp. sugar
1 Tbsp. dried oregano
½ tsp. freshly ground black pepper
¼ tsp. dried thyme
½ tsp. dried basil
2 tsp. dried parsley
2 tsp. salt
8 precooked brats
8 Italian rolls, sliced
Dill relish, or Italian pickled vegetables to serve (optional)

This is a wonderful menu for a hearty picnic!

DIRECTIONS:

1. Place chicken breasts in slow cooker.

2. In a separate bowl, combine the vinegar, oil, garlic, sugar, oregano, pepper, thyme, basil, parsley, and salt. Pour mixture over chicken breasts. Cover and cook on low for 6 hours.

3. Shred chicken with 2 forks. Add brats, cover, and cook on low for 2 additional hours.

4. Place brats in rolls and top with chicken and juices. Garnish with dill relish, if desired.

Cinque Beans

INGREDIENTS:

    1 16-oz. can pinto beans, rinsed and drained
    1 16-oz. can lima beans, rinsed and drained
    1 16-oz. can black beans, rinsed and drained
    1 16-oz. can dark red kidney beans, rinsed and drained
    16 oz. green beans, cut
    1 small onion, minced
    ½ cup white vinegar
    ⅓ cup sugar
    2 Tbsp. olive oil
    ½ tsp. salt
    ½ tsp. freshly ground black pepper

DIRECTIONS:

1. Put all beans and minced onion in slow cooker.

2. In separate bowl, whisk together vinegar, sugar, oil, salt, and pepper. Pour over beans and toss to combine.

3. Cover and cook on low for 2 hours.

We love Chicago for the brats and the Cubs... but we can't decide which is more fun!

World's Largest Crab Cake
and Warm & Tangy Coleslaw

World's Largest Crab Cake

INGREDIENTS:

1 lb. crabmeat
2½ cups panko (Japanese breadcrumbs), divided
2 Tbsp. fresh parsley, minced
2 Tbsp. fresh green onion, minced
4 eggs, beaten
1 Tbsp. lemon juice
1 tsp. dry mustard
1 tsp. Worcestershire sauce
¼ tsp. cayenne pepper
½ tsp. kosher salt

DIRECTIONS:

1. Grease inside of slow cooker. In a separate bowl, combine crabmeat, 1½ cups breadcrumbs, parsley, and green onion. Set aside.

2. In a second bowl, whisk together eggs, lemon juice, mustard, Worcestershire sauce, cayenne, and salt. Combine with crabmeat mixture and egg mixture using hands or wooden spoon. Form into one large cake and set in slow cooker.

3. Carefully press remaining cup breadcrumbs on top and sides. Cover and cook on high for 3 to 4 hours. Serve with Warm & Tangy Coleslaw.

Warm & Tangy Coleslaw

INGREDIENTS:

2 cups green cabbage, chopped
2 cups purple cabbage, chopped
¼ cup finely chopped onion
¼ cup olive oil
¼ cup white vinegar
½ cup water
¼ cup honey
1 tsp. salt
2 tsp. freshly ground black pepper

DIRECTIONS:

1. Put cabbage and onion in slow cooker. Toss to combine.

2. In separate bowl, whisk together olive oil, vinegar, water, honey, salt, and pepper. Pour over cabbage and toss to combine. Cover and cook on low for 2 to 3 hours. Serve over World's Largest Crab Cake.

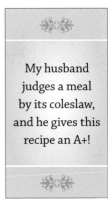

My husband judges a meal by its coleslaw, and he gives this recipe an A+!

Autumn Festival Stuffed Squash and Herbed Cauliflower

Autumn Festival Stuffed Squash

INGREDIENTS:

1 small onion, chopped
2 carrots, peeled and grated
2 fresh garlic cloves, peeled and minced
¾ lb. ground turkey, browned
1½ cups cooked long grain brown rice
4 small autumn squash
1 14.5 oz. jar tomato sauce
½ tsp. dried basil
½ tsp. dried oregano
½ tsp. dried thyme
½ cup asiago cheese, shredded

DIRECTIONS:

1. Cut the squash in half and scoop out the seeds. In a separate bowl mix onion, carrot, garlic, browned ground turkey, and rice; mix well to combine. Spoon the turkey mixture generously into each squash.

2. Transfer the squash, cut side up, into a greased slow cooker.

3. In a medium bowl, mix tomato sauce, basil, oregano, and thyme. Pour tomato mixture over the squash. Cover and cook on low for 4 to 5 hours.

4. Sprinkle with the cheese. Cover and cook an additional 20 minutes.

Herbed Cauliflower

INGREDIENTS:

1 head cauliflower
4 cloves garlic, minced
½ cup water
2 Tbsp. olive oil
½ tsp. freshly ground pepper
2 Tbsp. fresh parsley, minced
1 Tbsp. chives, chopped

DIRECTIONS:

1. Cut florets from the head of cauliflower. Place cauliflower, garlic, water, and olive oil in slow cooker. Cover and cook on low for 4 hours or until fork tender.

2. Drain off water. Toss with pepper, parsley, and chives.

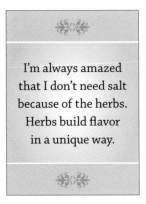

I'm always amazed
that I don't need salt
because of the herbs.
Herbs build flavor
in a unique way.

Frozen Cranberry Salad and Minnesota Wild Rice Soup

Frozen Cranberry Salad

INGREDIENTS:

  2 16-oz. cans whole cranberry sauce
  ½ cup cranberries, chopped
  1 20-oz. can crushed pineapple
  1 cup chopped walnuts, finely chopped
  2 cups plain yogurt

DIRECTIONS:

1. Combine all ingredients in slow cooker. Cover and freeze at least 5 hours.

2. Remove from freezer and let sit at room temperature at least 30 minutes before serving.

This salad is beautiful and richly flavored. It's always a big hit at my table!

Minnesota Wild Rice Soup

INGREDIENTS:

4 oz. wild rice, cooked
½ cup butter
1 clove garlic, minced
½ small fresh onion, peeled and cut small
3 stalks celery, chopped
3 medium carrots, peeled and chopped
1 cup flour
1 qt. chicken stock, preferably homemade
2 cups cooked fresh chicken, cut into ½-inch pieces
2 cups half-and-half
4 oz. slivered almonds

> This soup is even better the next day!

DIRECTIONS:

1. Melt butter in saucepan over medium heat. Add flour and stir to combine. Cook 30 seconds, then add garlic, onion, celery, and carrots. Transfer mixture to slow cooker.

2. Add cooked rice, chicken stock, and chicken to slow cooker. Cover and cook on low for 8 to 10 hours. Stir several times during cooking, and add half-and-half an hour before serving.

3. To serve, sprinkle slivered almonds over each bowl.

Shepherd's Pie and Sugar Snap Peas

Shepherd's Pie

INGREDIENTS:

1 lb. ground beef
8 oz. fresh mushrooms, chopped
1 small onion, chopped
2 cloves garlic, minced
1 tsp. salt
1 tsp. freshly ground black pepper
1 Tbsp. Worcestershire sauce
1 Tbsp. flour
½ cup vegetable stock
1 cup milk
½ cup corn
1 carrot, peeled and sliced
2 baking potatoes, peeled and cubed
⅛ cup green onion, chopped
2 cups shredded cheddar cheese, divided
1 tsp. salt
1 Tbsp. ground paprika

My English son-in-law says Shepherd's Pie is a classic dish at his home. It's become a classic in our home too!

DIRECTIONS:

1. Brown beef in skillet. Drain and transfer to slow cooker. Scatter mushrooms and onion over meat.

2. Combine garlic, salt, pepper, Worcestershire sauce, and flour in skillet. Cook 1 minute, stirring constantly. Add vegetable stock and milk. Let simmer until gravy thickens, 6 to 8 minutes, stirring occasionally. Pour gravy into slow cooker.

3. Sprinkle corn and carrots on top of gravy. In separate bowl, toss potatoes with green onion, 1 cup cheddar, and salt. Spread potatoes on top of corn and carrots. Top with remaining cup cheddar and sprinkle with paprika.

4. Cover and cook on low for 3 to 4 hours.

Sugar Snap Peas

INGREDIENTS:

1½ lbs. sugar snap peas
2 Tbsp. lemon juice
1 tsp. sugar
½ tsp. salt
½ tsp. pepper
1 lemon, sliced

DIRECTIONS:

1. Toss all ingredients except lemon together in slow cooker. Cover and cook on low for 2 hours.

2. Serve with sliced lemon on the side.

These sweet, bright green peas are the perfect accompaniment to a hearty shepherd's pie!

Ayam Kecap and Baked Mangoes

Ayam Kecap (Indonesian chicken in sweet soy sauce)

INGREDIENTS:

2 lbs. chicken breasts, cut into small cubes
¼ cup flour
¼ cup soy sauce
1 tsp. powdered ginger
8 oz. button mushrooms, sliced thin
8 garlic cloves, sliced thin
1 Tbsp. fresh grated ginger
6 Tbsp. hoisin sauce
4 Tbsp. water
2 Tbsp. oil
1 tsp. freshly ground black pepper
2 lemons, cut into wedges

DIRECTIONS:

1. In a medium bowl, whisk together flour, soy sauce, and powdered ginger. Mix well and add chicken. Stir to coat and let stand 30 minutes.

2. Transfer chicken mixture to greased slow cooker and add mushrooms, garlic, fresh ginger, hoisin sauce, water, oil, and black pepper. Mix well.

3. Cover and cook on low for 4 to 5 hours. To serve, squeeze a lemon wedge over each serving.

Baked Mangoes

INGREDIENTS:

6 mangoes, peeled and sliced
2 peaches, peeled and sliced
2 Tbsp. water
2 tsp. ground cinnamon
½ tsp. ground cardamom

DIRECTIONS:

1. Arrange mangoes and peaches in greased slow cooker. Pour water over fruit and sprinkle with cinnamon and cardamom.

2. Cover and cook on low for 2 hours.

Apricot Pistachio Bread and Pumpkin Soup

Apricot Pistachio Bread

INGREDIENTS:

- ¾ cup dried apricots, chopped
- 1½ cups boiling water
- ¼ cup olive oil
- 1 cup sugar
- 2 egg whites, beaten
- 1 Tbsp. vanilla
- 1⅓ cups flour
- 1⅓ cups whole wheat flour
- ⅛ tsp. salt
- 2 tsp. baking soda
- ½ tsp. baking powder
- ½ cup pistachio nuts, finely crushed

DIRECTIONS:

1. Place chopped apricots in a small bowl. Pour boiling water over apricots and set aside for 10 minutes to cool.

2. Combine olive oil and sugar in a separate bowl. Add in egg whites and vanilla and stir to combine. Stir in apricots and water.

3. In a separate bowl, mix flours, salt, baking soda, and baking powder. Gently stir dry ingredients into wet ingredients.

4. Lay several sheets of aluminum foil in slow cooker and grease with nonstick spray. Pour batter into pot. Sprinkle pistachio nuts on top. Cover and cook on high 1½ to 2½ hours.

Pumpkin Soup

INGREDIENTS:

2 3- to 4-lb. baking pumpkins
1 cup celery, chopped
6 cups chicken stock, preferably
    homemade
1 bay leaf
1 Tbsp. fresh basil, chopped

1 Tbsp. vegetable oil
1 cup half-and-half
1 Tbsp. vanilla
½ cup pumpkin seeds
½ cup dried cranberries
2 Tbsp. butter, melted

DIRECTIONS:

This soup's dramatic presentation will be the centerpiece of your meal!

1. Cut one of the pumpkins in half and remove the seeds and pulp. Discard. Scoop out flesh and put in slow cooker. Cover with chicken stock, celery, bay leaf, and basil.

2. Cover and cook in slow cooker on low for 4 hours or until tender.

3. Remove bay leaf. Purée contents of slow cooker in blender or food processor. Transfer pumpkin purée to separate bowl and rinse out slow cooker.

4. With a sharp knife, cut 3-inch circle around the stem of the second pumpkin. Remove seeds and pulp. Discard.

5. Brush inside of pumpkin lightly with melted butter and outside with vegetable oil. Place whole pumpkin in center of clean slow cooker and pour purée into the cavity. Cover and cook on low for 1 to 1½ hours.

6. Stir in half-and-half and vanilla. Cover and cook on low an additional 45 minutes.

7. To serve, take pumpkin out of slow cooker and set on plate. For individual servings, garnish by sprinkling dried cranberries and pumpkin seeds on top of soup.

Shrimp Creole and Orange-Butter Carrots

Shrimp Creole

INGREDIENTS:

1 lb. shrimp, peeled and deveined
4 cloves garlic, minced
1 large onion, chopped
1 6-oz. can tomato paste
1 14.5-oz can tomato sauce
1 cup water
2 stalks celery, chopped
¼ tsp. cayenne pepper
1 tsp. smoked paprika
1 tsp. salt
1 bay leaf

DIRECTIONS:

1. Combine garlic, onion, tomato paste, tomato sauce, water, celery, cayenne, paprika, salt, and bay leaf in slow cooker. Stir to combine. Cover and cook on low for 2 to 3 hours.

2. Add shrimp to slow cooker and toss gently to coat. Cook on low for 1 hour. Remove bay leaf before serving.

Orange-Butter Carrots

INGREDIENTS:

2 lbs. baby carrots
½ cup butter, melted
½ cup orange juice, freshly squeezed
1 tsp. salt
½ tsp. freshly ground pepper
1 Tbsp. orange zest

DIRECTIONS:

1. Combine carrots, melted butter, orange juice, salt, and pepper in slow cooker. Cover and cook on low for 4 hours.

2. To serve, sprinkle carrots with orange zest.

These meltingly tender carrots go well with almost any entrée.

Chicken Manicotti
and Parsley Soup

Chicken Manicotti

INGREDIENTS:

2 Tbsp. olive oil
1 fresh onion, peeled and chopped
1 28-oz can tomato sauce
1 tsp. garlic salt
1 tsp. dried oregano
1 tsp. dried basil
1 tsp. thyme
3 lbs. boneless skinless chicken breasts, cooked and shredded
14 manicotti shells, uncooked
½ cup water
1 cup shredded mozzarella cheese, divided
½ cup grated parmesan cheese
½ cup ricotta cheese

DIRECTIONS:

1. In large bowl, mix the olive oil, onion, tomato sauce, garlic salt, oregano, dried basil, and thyme. Pour ¾ cup sauce into slow cooker.

2. Pour ½ cup sauce into separate bowl and toss with shredded chicken, ¾ cup mozzarella, and ricotta. Fill each manicotti noodle with this mixture. Place the stuffed manicotti on top of sauce in slow cooker.

3. Mix water with remaining sauce in bowl. Pour sauce over manicotti, making sure to coat pasta completely. Cover and cook on low for 3 to 4 hours, or until pasta is tender when pierced with a fork.

4. Sprinkle with remaining ¼ cup mozzarella cheese and parmesan cheese. Cover and cook on low for an additional 30 minutes to melt cheese.

Parsley Soup

INGREDIENTS:

1 cup fresh parsley, chopped fine
2 Tbsp. olive oil
¼ cup flour
5 cups chicken stock, preferably homemade
2 cups water
1 medium onion, chopped
2 celery stalks, chopped
1 tsp. fresh basil, chopped
1 tsp. fresh cilantro, chopped
1 tsp. freshly ground pepper
4 oz. low-fat plain yogurt

This soup is a light but tasty accompaniment to a hearty Italian meal.

DIRECTIONS:

1. Chop vegetables and parsley, reserving several sprigs of parsley for garnish.

2. Heat olive oil in saucepan over medium-high heat until shimmering. Add flour and cook 30 seconds. Pour chicken stock and water into saucepan and stir until beginning to thicken, 8 to 10 minutes.

3. Pour thickened chicken stock into slow cooker. Mix in parsley, onion, celery, basil, cilantro, and pepper. Cover and cook on low for 6 to 8 hours.

4. To serve, dollop yogurt onto bowls of soup and add a sprig of parsley.

Brownies in a Mug
and Grapefruit Chicken

Brownies in a Mug

INGREDIENTS:

1½ squares unsweetened baking chocolate
½ cup butter
1 cup sugar
1 tsp. vanilla
2 eggs
½ cup flour
½ cup chopped walnuts (optional)
3 or 4 stoneware mugs that will fit
   inside slow cooker
1 pint vanilla ice cream
1 pint fresh seasonal berries

Brownies in a
Mug is the sort
of blow-you-
away dessert
your kids will
be talking
about for days!

DIRECTIONS:

1. Melt chocolate and butter in small saucepan. Pour into medium bowl and beat in sugar and vanilla. Add eggs; beat well. Stir in flour and walnuts, if desired.

2. Spray the inside of the mugs with nonstick spray. Fill each mug ⅓ full and place in the slow cooker. Pour ¼ cup water around the mugs.

3. Cover and cook on high for 1 to 2 hours. The brownies are fully cooked when they have doubled in size and pulled away slightly at the sides. Don't overcook—these are best when they're still a little gooey.

4. Lift each mug from the slow cooker with a potholder. Let cool several minutes and serve with ice cream and fresh berries.

Grapefruit Chicken

INGREDIENTS:

2 lbs. boneless, skinless chicken breasts
1 cup spinach leaves
1 grapefruit, peeled and sectioned
1 cup grapefruit juice
¼ cup white balsamic vinegar
¼ cup honey

DIRECTIONS:

1. Place chicken in greased slow cooker. Scatter spinach and grapefruit over top. In a separate bowl, mix together juice, vinegar, and honey. Pour mixture over grapefruit.

2. Cover and cook on low for 6 to 7 hours.

Chapter 5

Simple Meals: Making
Life a Little Easier

*As the rain and the snow come down from heaven,
and do not return to it without watering the earth
and making it bud and flourish, so that it yields
seed for the sower and bread for the eater, so is my
word that goes out from my mouth: It will not
return to me empty, but will accomplish what I
desire and achieve the purpose for which I sent it.*

Isaiah 55:10-11

Meatball Submarine Sandwiches and Triple Pepper Roast

Meatball Submarine Sandwiches

INGREDIENTS:

2 lbs. turkey or chicken meatballs, frozen or thawed
1 28-oz. can tomato sauce
1 tsp. dried basil
1 tsp. dried oregano
1 tsp. garlic salt
1 tsp. onion powder
8 oz. provolone cheese, sliced
8 Italian rolls
¼ cup grated parmesan cheese, optional

DIRECTIONS:

1. Combine tomato sauce, basil, oregano, garlic salt, and onion powder in greased slow cooker. Add meatballs and toss to coat.

2. Cover and cook on low for 5 to 6 hours.

3. Place a slice of provolone in each roll. Spoon meatballs and sauce on top of cheese. Sprinkle with grated parmesan or top with Triple Pepper Roast.

These are the perfect sandwiches for a Saturday lunch.

Triple Pepper Roast

INGREDIENTS:

2 green peppers, seeded and sliced
2 red peppers, seeded and sliced
2 yellow peppers, seeded and sliced
¼ cup extra-virgin olive oil

DIRECTIONS:

1. Pour olive oil into bottom of slow cooker. Add all the peppers and toss to coat.

2. Cover and cook on low for 5 to 6 hours.

Herbed Corn on the Cob and Sloppy Joes

Herbed Corn on the Cob

INGREDIENTS:

12 ears of corn, husk and silk removed
½ cup butter, softened
½ tsp. garlic salt
½ tsp. dry mustard
½ tsp. dried thyme
½ tsp. pepper
Aluminum foil

DIRECTIONS:

1. In small bowl, mix together softened butter, garlic salt, mustard, thyme, and pepper. Set aside.

2. Boil 2 qt. water in large saucepan. Add corn and boil for 4 minutes. Remove to paper towel-lined plate and let cool.

3. Spread butter mixture over each ear of corn and wrap separately in aluminum foil. Stack ears in slow cooker. Cover and cook on low for 2 hours.

This is the perfect menu for a summer evening!

Sloppy Joes

INGREDIENTS:

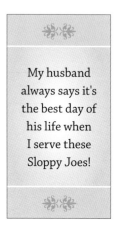

My husband always says it's the best day of his life when I serve these Sloppy Joes!

2 lbs. ground beef or turkey
1 onion, chopped
2 stalks celery, chopped
1 clove garlic, minced
1 6-oz. can tomato paste
1½ cups ketchup
1 Tbsp. apple cider vinegar
¼ cup brown sugar
½ tsp. salt
½ tsp. pepper
½ tsp. dry mustard powder
8 hamburger buns

DIRECTIONS:

1. Brown beef in large skillet. Drain and transfer to slow cooker.

2. Stir onion, celery, garlic, tomato paste, ketchup, cider vinegar, brown sugar, salt, pepper, and mustard into slow cooker. Cover and cook on low for 6 to 7 hours, then uncover and cook 1 additional hour.

3. To serve, spoon mixture onto hamburger buns.

Rosemary Chicken and Cooked Apple Slices

Rosemary Chicken

INGREDIENTS:

- ¼ cup olive oil
- 2 Tbsp. lemon juice
- 1 tsp. sugar
- 1 tsp. salt
- 2 lbs. boneless, skinless chicken breasts
- 1 Tbsp. chopped fresh rosemary
- 1 Tbsp. fresh oregano

DIRECTIONS:

1. Combine olive oil, lemon juice, sugar, and salt in large freezer bag. Add the chicken breasts and marinate 1 hour, flipping once.

2. Remove chicken breasts and discard marinade. Put breasts in slow cooker, sprinkling rosemary and oregano over top.

3. Cover and cook on low for 6 to 7 hours.

Cooked Apple Slices

INGREDIENTS:

6 apples, peeled and sliced
¼ cup sugar
2 tsp. cinnamon
3 Tbsp. real maple syrup

DIRECTIONS:

1. Put apple slices in slow cooker and sprinkle sugar and cinnamon over top. Drizzle maple syrup over apples.

2. Cover and cook on low for 2 to 3 hours.

Chili and Buttermilk Cornbread

Chili

INGREDIENTS:

1 lb. ground beef
1 onion, chopped
2 stalks celery, chopped
1 green bell pepper, seeded and chopped
1 14.5-oz. can tomato puree
1 28-oz. can diced tomatoes
1 15-oz. can kidney beans, rinsed and drained
1 15-oz. can black beans, rinsed and drained
1 15-oz. can cannellini beans, rinsed and drained
1 Tbsp. chili powder
1 tsp. garlic salt
1 tsp. dried oregano
½ tsp. freshly ground black pepper
¼ tsp. cayenne pepper
2 cups shredded cheddar cheese

DIRECTIONS:

1. Brown beef in large skillet. Drain and transfer to slow cooker.

2. Add all remaining ingredients except cheese to slow cooker and mix well. Cover and cook on low for 8 to 10 hours, stirring occasionally.

3. Top individual servings with cheese and serve with cornbread.

As a special treat for the kids, scoop the chili into ice cream cones!

Buttermilk Cornbread

INGREDIENTS:

1¼ cups flour
¾ cup cornmeal
½ cup sugar
¼ cup light brown sugar
2 tsp. baking powder
¼ tsp. baking soda
1 tsp. salt
2 eggs
1 cup buttermilk
½ cup butter, melted

To spice things up a bit, try this variation. Add 1 cup chopped onion, 3 or 4 chopped jalapeño peppers, and 2 cups shredded cheddar cheese to the batter. This is cornbread with a kick!

DIRECTIONS:

1. Combine flour, cornmeal, sugars, baking powder, baking soda, and salt in medium bowl.

2. Beat together egg, buttermilk, and melted butter in separate bowl. Pour into dry ingredients and mix until just combined.

3. Pour batter into greased slow cooker. Cover and cook on high for 2 to 3 hours. Cornbread is done when edges are brown and pull away from the sides. To serve, turn cornbread out onto a large platter or cutting board. Let cool at least 10 minutes before slicing.

Hot Turkey Sandwiches and Apple Cider Punch

Hot Turkey Sandwiches

INGREDIENTS:

1 lb. turkey cutlets
4 cups leftover mashed potatoes
1 10-oz. jar turkey gravy
2 tsp. paprika
Slices of soft whole grain bread
1 tsp. freshly ground pepper

DIRECTIONS:

1. Grease slow cooker and arrange turkey cutlets in bottom. Scoop mashed potatoes around the edges. Pour gravy over turkey and potatoes and sprinkle with paprika.

2. Cover and cook on low for 6 to 8 hours.

3. To serve, scoop turkey and potatoes over slices of bread and sprinkle with pepper.

This is a great way to use up leftover mashed potatoes!

Apple Cider Punch

INGREDIENTS:

1 gallon apple cider
1 qt. mango or papaya juice
1 qt. pomegranate juice
4 whole cloves
2 cinnamon sticks

DIRECTIONS:

1. Pour cider and juices into slow cooker. Stir in cloves and add cinnamon sticks.

2. Cover and heat on low for 2 to 3 hours. Ladle into mugs to serve.

Sweet & Sour Chicken

INGREDIENTS:

2 lbs. boneless, skinless chicken breasts
1 onion, cut into wedges
1 green bell pepper, seeded and sliced
1 carrot, peeled and sliced
1 tsp. salt
⅔ cup red wine vinegar
6 Tbsp. tomato sauce
6 Tbsp. pineapple juice
1 Tbsp. cornstartch
½ cup sugar
1 tsp. crushed red pepper flakes
1 20-oz. can pineapple chunks
Jasmine rice, to serve

After this homemade meal, you'll never settle for take-out again!

DIRECTIONS:

1. Cut chicken into bite-sized pieces and transfer to slow cooker. Add onion, pepper, and carrot.

2. In separate bowl, whisk together salt, vinegar, tomato sauce, pineapple juice, cornstarch, sugar, and red pepper flakes. Pour sauce over chicken and toss to coat.

3. Cover and cook on low for 5 to 7 hours. Add pineapple chunks and cook 30 minutes longer.

4. Serve over jasmine rice.

Hot & Sour Soup

INGREDIENTS:

2 qts. chicken broth, preferably homemade
8 oz. firm tofu, cubed
4 oz. ground pork
12 oz. mushrooms, sliced
⅓ cup bamboo shoots, diced
1 8-oz. can sliced water chestnuts
2 Tbsp. soy sauce
½ tsp. sugar
2 Tbsp. rice wine vinegar
¼ tsp. crushed red pepper flakes
2 Tbsp. cornstarch
3 Tbsp. water
1 tsp. sesame oil
2 green onions, chopped

DIRECTIONS:

1. Combine chicken broth, tofu, ground pork, mushrooms, bamboo shoots, water chestnuts, soy sauce, sugar, rice wine vinegar, and pepper flakes in slow cooker.

2. Mix cornstarch and water in small bowl. Stir mixture into soup. Cover and cook on low for 6 to 8 hours. Stir in sesame oil. Sprinkle green onion over individual bowls to serve.

Roasted Garlic Salad and Party Pizza

Roasted Garlic Salad

INGREDIENTS:

1 head garlic
3 Tbsp. olive oil, divided
Fresh salad greens, to serve

DIRECTIONS:

1. Slice off the top of the head of garlic so the cloves are exposed. Place garlic in slow cooker and drizzle 1 Tbsp. oil on top. Cover and cook on low for 6 to 7 hours, or until the garlic is completely soft.

2. Separate the head into individual cloves and squeeze out garlic. In small bowl, mix garlic with 2 Tbsp. olive oil. Toss oil with salad greens thoroughly, until leaves are just lightly coated.

Party Pizza

INGREDIENTS:

3 Tbsp. olive oil, divided
1 can refrigerated pizza dough
1 cup tomato sauce
1 6-oz. can tomato paste
1 clove garlic, minced
1 tsp. salt
2 tsp. oregano
2 tsp. basil
¼ tsp. freshly ground black
    pepper
6 oz. pepperoni
1 lb. shredded mozzarella cheese

You can use any toppings you like on this pizza. My family also enjoys black olives, sliced mushrooms, and sausage.

DIRECTIONS:

1. Pour 1 Tbsp. olive oil in bottom of slow cooker. Stretch out pizza dough and lay down in slow cooker.

2. In small bowl, combine tomato sauce, tomato paste, 2 Tbsp. olive oil, garlic, salt, oregano, basil, and pepper. Spread sauce over crust.

3. Top with mozzarella and pepperoni. Cover and cook on low for 3 to 4 hours.

Fish Sticks and Captain Mac

Fish Sticks

INGREDIENTS:

1½ lbs. fresh whitefish fillets
½ cup bread crumbs
2 Tbsp. butter, melted
¼ tsp. salt
½ tsp. freshly ground black pepper
¼ tsp. paprika

DIRECTIONS:

1. Grease slow cooker and arrange fillets in bottom of pot.

2. Put breadcrumbs in small bowl and add melted butter, salt, pepper, and paprika. Toss with a fork to combine. Spoon mixture over fish, pressing with fingers to adhere.

3. Cover and cook on high 1 to 1½ hours.

I like to serve these with cocktail sauce for the grownups and ketchup for the kids.

Captain Mac

INGREDIENTS:

1 lb. elbow macaroni
6 oz. colby cheese, shredded
6 oz. asiago cheese, shredded
6 oz. sharp cheddar cheese, shredded
4 Tbsp. butter
¾ cup milk
2 eggs, beaten
1 tsp. salt
1 tsp. freshly ground black pepper
½ tsp. dry mustard

DIRECTIONS:

1. Cook macaroni according to package directions until just shy of al dente. Drain and transfer to slow cooker. Mix in butter and cheese.

2. In separate bowl, whisk together milk, eggs, salt, pepper, and dry mustard. Pour over macaroni. Cover and cook on low for 2 to 3 hours.

If there's a more satisfying comfort food out there, I haven't found it yet!

Apple, Grape, & Walnut Chicken and Hot Mocha Frappes

Apple, Grape, & Walnut Chicken

INGREDIENTS:

- 1 cup Greek yogurt
- 1 Tbsp. honey
- ½ tsp. nutmeg
- ½ tsp. cinnamon
- 2 lbs. boneless, skinless chicken breasts
- 2 apples, peeled and chopped
- 1 cup chopped walnuts
- 2 cups halved grapes

DIRECTIONS:

1. In medium bowl, stir together yogurt, honey, nutmeg, and cinnamon. Dip each breast in yogurt and lay inside greased slow cooker. Spoon any additional yogurt over chicken.

2. Scatter apples, walnuts, and grapes over chicken. Cover and cook on high for 3 to 4 hours.

Hot Mocha Frappes

INGREDIENTS:

4 cups brewed coffee
1 12-oz. can evaporated milk
2 cups milk
2 tsp. vanilla
1 cup semisweet chocolate chips
½ cup white chocolate chips

DIRECTIONS:

1. Pour all ingredients into slow cooker and stir to combine. Cover and cook on low, stirring occasionally, for 3 to 4 hours.

2. Whisk thoroughly and ladle into coffee cups to serve.

Sausage-Shrimp Jambalaya and Deep South Raisins

Sausage-Shrimp Jambalaya

INGREDIENTS:

- 1 lb. smoked sausage, sliced into ½-inch pieces
- 2 cups cooked rice
- 1 14.5-oz. can diced tomatoes
- 1 stalk celery, chopped
- 1 green bell pepper, seeded and chopped
- 2 cloves garlic, minced
- 10 oz. fresh or frozen okra
- 2 tsp. Worcestershire sauce
- ½ tsp. hot pepper sauce
- 2 cups chicken broth
- 1 Tbsp. lemon juice
- ½ tsp. salt
- ½ tsp. freshly ground black pepper
- ¼ tsp. cayenne pepper
- 1 tsp. dried oregano
- 1 tsp. dried thyme
- 1 lb. shrimp, peeled and deveined

DIRECTIONS:

1. Add the sausage, cooked rice, tomatoes, celery, bell pepper, garlic, and okra to the slow cooker. Toss to combine.

2. In separate bowl, mix together the Worcestershire sauce, hot pepper sauce, chicken broth, lemon juice, salt, pepper, cayenne, oregano, and thyme. Pour over contents of slow cooker and stir to combine.

3. Cover and cook on low for 3 to 5 hours. Add the shrimp in the last hour of cooking time.

Deep South Raisins

INGREDIENTS:

2 vanilla beans
4 cups water
1 cup sugar
¼ cup flour
1 tsp. salt
2 Tbsp. butter
2 Tbsp. lemon juice, freshly squeezed
2 cups raisins
2 cups golden raisins

DIRECTIONS:

1. Using a sharp knife, cut open the vanilla beans and carefully scrape out the seeds. Transfer seeds and pods to slow cooker. Add water, sugar, flour, salt, butter, and lemon juice. Mix well, and then stir in raisins.

2. Cover and cook on low for 3 to 4 hours, stirring several times during cooking. Remove vanilla bean pods before serving.

Italian Sausage Hoagie and Hoagie Sauce

Italian Sausage Hoagie

INGREDIENTS:

2 lbs. 8-inch Italian sausage links, uncooked
2 green peppers, seeded and sliced
1 cup apple juice
Italian rolls, for serving

DIRECTIONS:

1. Arrange sausages and peppers in slow cooker. Pour apple juice over top. Cover and cook on low for 6 to 7 hours.

2. To serve, place sausage in cut Italian roll and add a few green peppers. Top each sausage with Italian Hoagie Sauce.

Hoagie Sauce

INGREDIENTS:

2 Tbsp. olive oil
1 tsp. white sugar
1 tsp. garlic powder
1 Tbsp. onion flakes
4 oz. mushrooms, sliced
1 tsp. dried basil
1 Tbsp. dried oregano
1 28-oz. can tomato sauce
1 6-oz. can tomato paste
1 tsp. crushed red pepper flakes

DIRECTIONS:

1. Combine all ingredients in slow cooker. Cover and cook on low for 3 to 4 hours.

2. To serve, spoon over Italian Sausage Hoagies.

Chapter 6

Bulk Bargains, Brilliant Meals

*When one of those at the table with him heard
this, he said to Jesus, "Blessed is the one who
will eat at the feast in the kingdom of God."*

LUKE 14:15

Spaghetti Night
and Italian Bread Basket

Spaghetti Night

INGREDIENTS:

1 lb. ground Italian sausage
8 oz. mushrooms
1 28-oz. can diced tomatoes
1 28-oz. can crushed tomatoes
1 6-oz. can tomato paste
1 onion, minced
2 cloves garlic, minced
½ tsp. crushed red pepper flakes
2 tsp. dried oregano
2 tsp. dried basil
2 tsp. dried thyme
1 tsp. salt
2 lbs. spaghetti, to serve

There are always requests for seconds when this simple but delicious meal is on the table!

DIRECTIONS:

1. Brown sausage in skillet over medium heat. Drain and transfer to slow cooker. Add mushrooms, diced and crushed tomatoes, tomato paste, onion, garlic, pepper flakes, oregano, basil, thyme, and salt.

2. Cover and cook on low for 6 to 7 hours, stirring occasionally. Serve over cooked spaghetti.

Italian Bread Basket

INGREDIENTS:

1 bag of bread dough rolls, in freezer section
2 Tbsp. olive oil
1 tsp. garlic salt
1 tsp. thyme
1 tsp. basil
1 tsp. oregano
1 tsp. sugar
½ tsp. salt
½ tsp. freshly ground black pepper
1 Tbsp. grated parmesan cheese

DIRECTIONS:

1. Drizzle olive oil in bottom of slow cooker. Add rolls, turning once to coat.

2. In small bowl, combine garlic salt, thyme, basil, oregano, sugar, salt, and pepper. Sprinkle spice mixture over rolls. Cover and cook on low for 3 hours.

3. Sprinkle parmesan over rolls in last half hour before serving.

Kraut & Brats
and Potatoes au Gratin

Kraut & Brats

INGREDIENTS:

8 bratwurst links, uncooked
1 14-oz. can sauerkraut, rinsed and drained
2 apples, peeled and chopped
3 strips bacon, cooked and crumbled
¼ cup packed brown sugar
1 small onion, chopped
1 tsp. dry mustard
1 tsp. Worcestershire sauce
¼ cup apple juice
8 brat buns, split

DIRECTIONS:

1. Set brats in slow cooker.

2. In separate bowl, combine sauerkraut, apples, bacon, brown sugar, onion, mustard, Worcestershire sauce, and apple juice. Spoon mixture over brats. Cover and cook on low 4 to 6 hours, or until brats are no longer pink.

3. Place brats in buns and top with sauerkraut.

Potatoes au Gratin

INGREDIENTS:

> 6 baking potatoes, sliced into ¼-inch rounds
> 1 12-oz. can evaporated milk
> 1 cup chicken broth
> 2 shallots, minced
> 1 tsp. salt
> ¼ tsp. cayenne pepper
> 1 tsp. dry mustard
> 1 cup shredded cheddar cheese

DIRECTIONS:

1. Put potato slices in large saucepan and cover with water. Bring to boil and cook 10 minutes. Drain. Arrange potatoes in bottom of slow cooker.

2. In separate bowl, whisk together evaporated milk, broth, shallots, salt, cayenne, and mustard. Pour over potatoes. Cover and cook on low for 6 to 8 hours.

3. In the last hour of cooking, scatter cheddar over top of potatoes.

To give this an extra kick, try substituting pepper jack cheese for the cheddar!

Sweet & Sour Hot Broccoli Salad and Fruity White Fish

Sweet & Sour Hot Broccoli Salad

INGREDIENTS:

2 heads broccoli, cut into florets
2 green onions, chopped
4 cups halved red grapes
¾ cup chopped walnuts
¼ cup raisins
3 strips turkey bacon, cooked and crumbled
2 Tbsp. sugar
¼ cup apple cider vinegar

DIRECTIONS:

1. Toss broccoli, onions, grapes, walnuts, raisins, and bacon in slow cooker.

2. In small bowl, combine sugar and vinegar. Pour over broccoli mixture and toss to coat.

3. Cover and cook on low for 2 to 4 hours.

This is the perfect salad to take to a barbecue or potluck. You'll love the sweet and sour combination!

Fruity White Fish

INGREDIENTS:

2 lbs. fresh whitefish fillets
1 cup best-quality fresh salsa, available in produce section
½ cup raspberries
2 kiwis, peeled and sliced
½ cup dry wasabi peas

DIRECTIONS:

1. Grease slow cooker and arrange fish in bottom.

2. Drain excess liquid from salsa. Mix with raspberries, kiwi, and wasabi peas. Spoon fruit mixture over the fish.

3. Cover and cook on high for 1½ to 2 hours.

The salsa and fruit topping on this dish is simply unbeatable!

Bean Soup

INGREDIENTS:

1 lb. ground turkey
3 cups chicken stock, preferably homemade
2 carrots, peeled and chopped
1 24-oz. can white navy beans, rinsed and drained
1 clove garlic, minced
1 4-oz. can chopped green chilies
1 tsp. cumin

DIRECTIONS:

1. Brown ground turkey in skillet set over medium-high heat. Drain and transfer to slow cooker.

2. Add all remaining ingredients to slow cooker. Cover and cook on low for 8 to 10 hours. Serve with hearty sourdough bread.

Peanut Butter Chocolate Pudding

INGREDIENTS:

1 cup flour
1¼ cups sugar, divided
6 Tbsp. cocoa powder, divided
1 tsp. baking powder
½ cup milk
1 Tbsp. vegetable oil
1 tsp. vanilla
¾ cup peanut butter chips
2 cups boiling water
½ cup creamy peanut butter
1 qt. vanilla ice cream

DIRECTIONS:

1. In medium bowl, mix together flour, ½ cup sugar, 2 Tbsp. cocoa powder, baking powder, milk, vegetable oil, and vanilla. Fold in peanut butter chips. Spread mixture on bottom of greased slow cooker.

2. In small bowl, mix together remaining ¾ cup sugar and ¼ cup cocoa powder. Set aside.

3. Stir boiling water into peanut butter. Pour into sugar and cocoa mixture and whisk to combine. Pour this mixture over batter in slow cooker.

4. Cover and cook on high 1 to 2 hours. Spoon over vanilla ice cream to serve.

Sweet & Sour Wings and Asian Vegetables

Sweet & Sour Wings

INGREDIENTS:

2½ cups of water
½ tsp. salt
1½ cups white sugar
⅔ cup apple cider vinegar
½ cup ketchup
1 tsp. soy sauce
⅓ cup pineapple juice
¼ cup cornstarch
3½ lbs. chicken wings, fresh or frozen

DIRECTIONS:

1. In a medium bowl, whisk together all ingredients except chicken.

2. Place chicken wings in slow cooker and pour sauce over top. Cover and cook on low for 5 to 7 hours.

This is a not-too-spicy alternative to hot wings that's sure to be a hit with your family. Add some kick with a pinch of cayenne or some chopped chilies if your family wants more heat.

Asian Vegetables

INGREDIENTS:

1 cup sliced bamboo shoots
1 15-oz. can baby corn, rinsed and drained
1 cup water chestnuts, thinly sliced
½ cup pineapple juice
1 tsp. freshly ground black pepper
1 tsp. sesame oil
1 Tbsp. sesame seeds, to serve

DIRECTIONS:

1. Combine bamboo shoots, corn, and water chestnuts in slow cooker. Pour pineapple juice over top and sprinkle with pepper. Cover and cook on low for 4 hours.

2. Sprinkle with sesame oil and toss to lightly coat. Scatter sesame seeds over top to serve.

Bread Pudding with Vanilla Sauce and Wholesome Lentil Soup

Bread Pudding

INGREDIENTS:

4 cups French bread cubes, toasted
2 eggs
2½ cups milk
¾ cup sugar
¼ tsp. cinnamon
¼ tsp. nutmeg
¼ tsp. salt
1 tsp. vanilla
2 Tbsp. butter, melted
½ cup raisins or dried cherries (optional)

For an extra treat, try this recipe with crumbled donuts instead of bread.

DIRECTIONS:

1. Grease slow cooker and add bread cubes. In a small bowl, whisk together the eggs, milk, sugar, cinnamon, nutmeg, salt, vanilla, and melted butter. Pour this mixture over the bread cubes. Add raisins or cherries over top if desired.

2. Cover and cook on low for 5 to 6 hours. Top with vanilla sauce to serve.

Vanilla Sauce

INGREDIENTS:

1 cup sugar
2 Tbsp. flour
¼ tsp. nutmeg
⅛ tsp. allspice
1 cup water
2 Tbsp. butter
1 tsp. vanilla

DIRECTIONS:

1. In a small saucepan, mix together sugar, flour, nutmeg, and allspice. Add water slowly, whisking constantly so that no lumps form.

2. Bring to a simmer and boil until clear and thickened. Remove from heat and add butter and vanilla. Whisk until combined and serve over bread pudding.

Wholesome Lentil Soup

INGREDIENTS:

1 lb. ground beef
1 medium onion, chopped
1 clove garlic, minced
4 ounces mushrooms, sliced
1 14.5-oz. can stewed tomatoes
1 stalk celery, chopped
1 large carrot, peeled and sliced
6 oz. dried lentils
3 qts. beef stock
2 cups water
1 bay leaf
2 tsp. salt
¼ tsp. freshly ground pepper
2 Tbsp. fresh parsley, chopped

For a foolproof soup, lentils are the easiest legume to work with.

DIRECTIONS:

1. Brown beef in skillet over medium high. Drain and transfer to slow cooker. Add chopped onions to skillet and cook until just softened, 3 to 5 minutes. Transfer to slow cooker and add garlic, mushrooms, tomatoes, celery, carrots, lentils, beef stock, water, bay leaf, salt, and pepper.

2. Cover and cook on low for 8 to 10 hours. To serve, scatter parsley over individual servings.

Lobster Pasta
and Corn Soufflé

Lobster Pasta

INGREDIENTS:

1 lb. lobster meat, cooked and flaked
16 oz. bowtie pasta
1 cup red grapes, halved
1 cup green grapes, halved
1 stalk celery, chopped
½ cup green peas
1 4-oz. jar pimentos, drained
¼ cup olive oil
1 tsp. salt
1 tsp. freshly ground black pepper
1 Tbsp. fresh dill, chopped
1 tsp. paprika

DIRECTIONS:

1. Prepare pasta according to package directions until just shy of al dente. Drain and transfer to greased slow cooker.

2. In a medium bowl, combine lobster meat, grapes, celery, peas, pimentos, olive oil, salt, pepper, and dill. Add to slow cooker and toss gently to combine.

3. Sprinkle paprika over top of casserole. Cover and cook on low for 4 hours.

Corn Soufflé

INGREDIENTS:

4 eggs, separated
3 cups fresh corn, cut from cob
1 cup milk
1 Tbsp. flour
1 tsp. salt
1 tsp. freshly ground pepper
⅓ cup Romano cheese, grated

DIRECTIONS:

1. Combine egg yolks, corn, milk, flour, salt, and pepper in blender. Blend until smooth.

2. In separate mixing bowl, beat egg whites until stiff. Fold blended corn mixture into eggs, then transfer mixture to greased slow cooker.

3. Sprinkle cheese over top. Cover and cook on low for 2 to 4 hours.

Wrapped Dover Sole and Wild Rice

Wrapped Dover Sole

INGREDIENTS:

12 oz. mango salsa
1 cup plain bread crumbs, toasted
¼ cup fresh lemon juice, freshly squeezed
½ tsp. pepper
2 lbs. Dover Sole (3- to 6-oz. fillets)
Corn tortillas

DIRECTIONS:

1. In a medium bowl, combine mango salsa, bread crumbs, lemon juice, and pepper.

2. Lay each fillet inside a tortilla and top with salsa mixture. Wrap tortilla around fish and close seam with a toothpick. Arrange in bottom of greased slow cooker.

3. Cover and cook on high for 1 to 2 hours.

This is the perfect dish for a summer evening. The fish and mango salsa complement each other perfectly!

Wild Rice

INGREDIENTS:

   2 cups uncooked wild rice
   ½ cup celery, chopped
   ½ cup button mushrooms, sliced
   2 Tbsp. olive oil
   5 cups chicken or vegetable stock

DIRECTIONS:

   1. Combine all ingredients in slow cooker. Stir well, then cover and cook on low for 6 to 8 hours.

   2. Fluff with a fork before serving.

For variety, try adding a sprig of rosemary and a few lavender buds to the rice.

Whole-in-One Chicken

INGREDIENTS:

1 4-5 lb. whole chicken, cleaned
2 stalks celery, cut in half horizontally
1 small onion, quartered
1 lemon, halved
1 bay leaf
1 tsp. salt
2 tsp. freshly ground black pepper

DIRECTIONS:

1. Stuff cavity of chicken with celery, onion, lemon, and bay leaf. Place chicken in bottom of greased slow cooker. Scatter any vegetables that don't fit inside the cavity around the chicken.

2. Sprinkle salt and pepper on top of chicken. Cover and cook on low for 7 hours.

3. To serve, empty chicken cavity of celery, onion, and lemon and carve.

Thyme Out Asparagus Bundles

INGREDIENTS:

 1 bunch green onions
 1½ lbs. asparagus spears
 2 tsp. olive oil
 2 Tbsp. fresh thyme, chopped
 1 tsp. freshly ground pepper
 1 orange, unpeeled and sliced very thin

DIRECTIONS:

1. Slit each green onion and cut into two long strips. Snap woody ends off asparagus and tie 3 spears at a time into bundles, using green onion as the string. Place bundles in bottom of slow cooker.

2. Drizzle olive oil over asparagus. Sprinkle with thyme and pepper. Arrange orange slices over bundles.

3. Cover and cook on low for 3 to 4 hours.

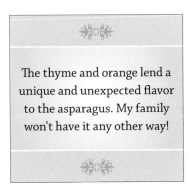

The thyme and orange lend a unique and unexpected flavor to the asparagus. My family won't have it any other way!

Tuna with Mustard Dill Sauce and Southern-Style Green Beans

Tuna with Mustard Dill Sauce

INGREDIENTS:

½ cup mayonnaise
2 Tbsp. fresh parsley leaves, minced
2 Tbsp. Dijon mustard
2 Tbsp. fresh dill weed, minced
1 Tbsp. lemon juice, freshly squeezed
1 tsp. salt
1 tsp. freshly ground black pepper
1 2-lb. tuna fillet
2 Tbsp. extra-virgin olive oil
2 tsp. freshly ground black pepper

This delicious sauce is perfect over the rich but delicate tuna. Make sure to use fresh dill here— it really makes a difference.

DIRECTIONS:

1. In a small bowl, mix together mayonnaise, parsley, mustard, dill weed, lemon juice, salt, and pepper. Cover bowl with plastic wrap and place in refrigerator until ready to use.

2. Rub tuna with olive oil and sprinkle with pepper. Place skin-side down onto bottom of greased slow cooker.

3. Cover and cook on low for 1 to 2 hours, until fish flakes with a fork. Serve with the chilled mustard dill sauce.

Southern-Style Green Beans

INGREDIENTS:

1½ lbs. green beans, trimmed
3 slices turkey bacon, cut in small pieces
1 Tbsp. olive oil
2 Tbsp. water
1 tsp. freshly ground black pepper
1 tsp. garlic salt

DIRECTIONS:

1. Put green beans and bacon in slow cooker and toss with oil until lightly coated. Pour water over top and sprinkle with pepper and garlic salt.

2. Cover and cook for 3 to 4 hours on low.

Bacon-Wrapped Chicken and Frozen Fruit Salad

Bacon-Wrapped Chicken

INGREDIENTS:

4 boneless, skinless chicken breasts
8 asparagus spears
1 green apple, cored and sliced
¼ cup pesto
1 Tbsp. olive oil
1 tsp. lemon juice
4 strips bacon
½ tsp. dried basil
½ tsp. dried oregano
¼ cup parmesan cheese, grated
1 tsp. freshly ground black pepper

DIRECTIONS:

1. Pound the chicken with a mallet to ½-inch thickness. Spoon 1 Tbsp. pesto over each breast, place two asparagus spears and one or two apple slices in the middle of the pesto.

2. Sprinkle olive oil and lemon juice over asparagus and apples. Roll chicken around asparagus and apples tightly. Wrap a strip of bacon around each roll and secure seam with a toothpick. Place chicken in bottom of greased slow cooker.

3. In small bowl, mix together basil, oregano, cheese, and pepper. Sprinkle mixture over chicken. Cover and cook on low for 6 to 8 hours.

Frozen Fruit Salad

INGREDIENTS:

2 cups buttermilk
1 cup sugar
½ tsp. vanilla
½ tsp. almond extract
1 Tbsp. grated orange zest
1 cup sliced strawberries
2 cups watermelon balls
1 cup blueberries
2 pears, peeled and chopped
2 tsp. lemon juice

DIRECTIONS:

1. In medium bowl, whisk together buttermilk, sugar, vanilla, almond extract, and orange zest.

2. Prepare fruit, sprinkling lemon juice over pears. Put fruit in slow cooker and pour buttermilk mixture over top. Toss gently to coat.

3. Put slow cooker in freezer and freeze at least 4 hours. Let stand at room temperature 15 minutes before serving.

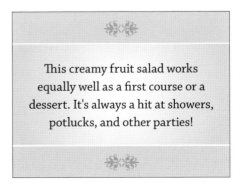

This creamy fruit salad works equally well as a first course or a dessert. It's always a hit at showers, potlucks, and other parties!

French Dip Sandwiches and Key Lime Dip

French Dip Sandwiches

INGREDIENTS:

- 1 4-lb. boneless beef roast
- 1 small onion, quartered
- ¼ cup soy sauce
- 2 cups beef stock
- 1 bay leaf
- 3 whole black peppercorns
- 2 sprigs fresh rosemary
- 1 tsp. dried thyme
- 1 tsp. garlic powder
- 8 crusty French rolls

This "double dip" menu will be a huge hit at your next party or dinner. You won't believe the succulent flavor of the beef jus!

DIRECTIONS:

1. Trim fat from roast and place meat in slow cooker. Arrange quartered onions around roast.

2. In medium bowl, combine soy sauce, beef stock, bay leaf, peppercorns, rosemary, thyme, and garlic powder. Pour into slow cooker. Add enough water to almost cover roast. Cover and cook on low for 10 to 12 hours, or until meat is very tender.

3. Remove meat from broth. Shred with forks and distribute on French rolls for sandwiches.

4. Pour jus through fine mesh strainer and discard solids. Serve jus alongside sandwiches for dipping.

Key Lime Dip

INGREDIENTS:

    5 egg yolks, beaten
    2 14-oz. cans sweetened condensed milk
    ¾ cup key lime juice
    1 Tbsp. lime zest
    Pretzels, to serve
    Graham crackers, to serve
    Fruit, cut ready to serve

DIRECTIONS:

1. Lightly zest the lime, being sure to avoid the bitter white pith. Place zest in medium bowl and add egg yolks. Whisk about 2 minutes, or until tinted light green. Beat in condensed milk and lime juice.

2. Transfer mixture to slow cooker. Cover and cook on low for 2 hours. Serve with pretzels, graham crackers, and cut fruit for dipping.

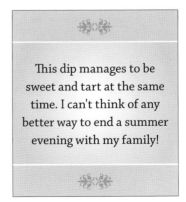

This dip manages to be sweet and tart at the same time. I can't think of any better way to end a summer evening with my family!

Chapter 7

Parties, Barbecues, and Gatherings

*Do not forget to show hospitality to strangers,
for by so doing some people have shown
hospitality to angels without knowing it.*

HEBREWS 13:2

Loaded Baked Potatoes and Tex-Mex Turkey Breast

Loaded Baked Potatoes

INGREDIENTS:

5 baking potatoes
2 cups shredded sharp cheddar cheese, divided
¾ cup plain yogurt
½ cup milk
¾ cup Thousand Island dressing
2 oz. fresh green onions, chopped
½ tsp. chili powder
4 strips turkey bacon, cooked and crumbled

DIRECTIONS:

1. Preheat oven to 400°. Set potatoes on baking sheet and cook 1 hour. Remove and let stand 5 minutes.

2. Slit the potatoes halfway so they open on a "hinge." Scoop out the potato flesh into a medium bowl. Mix in 1 cup cheese, yogurt, milk, dressing, green onion, and chili powder. Blend well, then stuff mixture back into the potato jackets.

3. Place potatoes in slow cooker and scatter bacon over top. Cover and cook on low for 2 to 3 hours.

4. Sprinkle remaining cup of cheese over potatoes and cook 30 additional minutes.

Tex-Mex Turkey Breast

INGREDIENTS:

1 5-lb. turkey breast
¼ cup extra virgin olive oil
2 cloves garlic, minced
1 small onion, minced
¾ cup ketchup
1 cup water
2 Tbsp. cider vinegar
¼ cup honey
1 tsp. chili powder
2 tsp. fresh oregano
1 tsp. Worcestershire sauce
½ tsp. ground cumin
½ tsp. dry mustard
½ tsp. liquid smoke

My daughter-
in-law won over
the family with
this recipe!

DIRECTIONS:

1. Mix olive oil, garlic, onion, ketchup, water, vinegar, honey, chili powder, oregano, Worcestershire sauce, cumin, dry mustard, and liquid smoke in large bowl. Whisk until combined.

2. Lay turkey in sauce, turning several times to coat. Cover and refrigerate overnight.

3. Remove turkey from marinade and place in slow cooker. Pour marinade over top of breast. Cover and cook on high for 8 hours, basting with juices several times during cooking.

Fruity Beef Brisket and Beef Brisket Topping

Fruity Beef Brisket

INGREDIENTS:

- 1 4-lb. beef brisket
- ½ cup grated onion
- 1 cup apple, peach, or pear juice
- 2 bay leaves
- ½ lb. plums
- ½ lb. dried apricots
- 2 lbs. rutabagas, peeled and cut into 1-inch cubes

DIRECTIONS:

1. Place the brisket fat side down in the slow cooker and rub grated onion over top. Pour juice around brisket and add bay leaves. Cover and cook on low for 5 hours, basting occasionally with juices.

2. Add the plums, apricots, and rutabagas. Cover and cook on low for 3 additional hours, or until the brisket and rutabagas are tender, but not too soft.

3. Let the meat rest for at least 30 minutes before slicing. To serve, arrange slices on platter and ladle Beef Brisket Topping over top.

Beef Brisket Topping

INGREDIENTS:

1 small onion, chopped
3 cloves garlic, minced
1 stalk celery, chopped
1 14.5-oz. can tomato sauce
1 Tbsp. white vinegar
¼ cup packed brown sugar
1½ tsp. Worcestershire sauce

DIRECTIONS:

1. Combine all ingredients in slow cooker. Cover and cook on low for 6 to 8 hours.

2. To serve, spoon sauce onto sliced beef brisket.

I love to serve the Beef Brisket and sauce on hearty kaiser rolls. It's a great dish for the big game!

Raspberry Ginger Ale Sponge Cupcakes and Rosehip Herbal Tea

Raspberry Ginger Ale Sponge Cupcakes

INGREDIENTS FOR CUPCAKES:

1 cup sugar
½ cup butter, softened
2 eggs
2 tsp. vanilla
1½ cups flour
1¾ tsp. baking powder
½ cup raspberry ginger ale

INGREDIENTS FOR FROSTING:

½ cup butter
4 cups powdered sugar
1 tsp. vanilla
¼ cup milk
1 dozen raspberries

There are few hours in life more agreeable than the hour dedicated to the ceremony known as afternoon tea.

Henry James

DIRECTIONS:

1. Cream the butter and sugar in a medium bowl. Beat in the eggs one at a time, stirring well after each addition, then add vanilla. Combine flour and baking powder, then add to creamed mixture. Stir to combine, then pour in the ginger ale. Batter will froth at first, but will come together with stirring.

2. Pour batter into aluminum foil cupcake holders, filling halfway. Set the cupcake holders into the slow cooker and cook on high for 2 to 3 hours, watching closely in the last hour of cooking.

3. For frosting, cream butter in a mixing bowl. Beat in sugar and vanilla. Pour in milk and beat until frosting reaches desired consistency. Frost cooled cupcakes and dot each with a raspberry.

Rosehip Herbal Tea

INGREDIENTS:

1 gallon water
½ cup dried or fresh rosehips
7 whole cloves
Honey, to taste

DIRECTIONS:

1. Pour water into slow cooker. Steep rose hips and cloves in water for 1 hour. If you don't have a steeper, put herbs in center of coffee filter and secure with a twist tie.

2. Cover and cook on low for 4 to 6 hours.

3. Sweeten individual servings of tea with honey, if desired, and serve with cupcakes.

I love to sip this tea with my daughters on lazy afternoons.

Hummus
and Baba Ghannoug

Hummus

INGREDIENTS:

2 15-oz. cans garbanzo beans
2 cloves garlic, minced
¼ cup lemon juice, freshly squeezed
½ cup tahini paste
1 Tbsp. fresh parsley, finely chopped
1 green onion, chopped
½ red bell pepper, seeded and chopped
Pita bread, broccoli florets, cauliflower florets, and blanched
green beans, to serve

DIRECTIONS:

1. Mash the garbanzo beans in bottom of slow cooker. Mix in the garlic, lemon juice, tahini, and parsley. Stir in green onions and red bell pepper.

2. Cover and cook on low for 1 hour. Serve with pita bread and assorted vegetables.

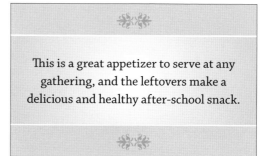

This is a great appetizer to serve at any gathering, and the leftovers make a delicious and healthy after-school snack.

Baba Ghannoug

INGREDIENTS:

1 eggplant
2 cloves fresh garlic, peeled and minced
¼ cup lemon juice, freshly squeezed
2 Tbsp. tahini paste
¼ cup parsley, chopped
1 tsp. salt
1 tsp. freshly ground pepper

DIRECTIONS:

1. Using a fork, pierce several holes in eggplant. Place in slow cooker. Cover and cook on high for 3 hours, or until flesh is soft when squeezed.

2. Remove eggplant to plate and let cool. When cool enough to handle, peel away skin and discard. Place the eggplant flesh in a strainer and drain for 10 minutes.

3. In a food processor, combine garlic, lemon juice, tahini, parsley, salt, and freshly ground pepper; pulse to combine. Add the eggplant flesh and pulse until smooth. Serve with pita bread and assorted vegetables.

Chili Cinnamon Nuts and Chicago Firehouse Chili

Chili Cinnamon Nuts

INGREDIENTS:

3 12-oz. cans cocktail peanuts
¼ cup butter, melted
2 tsp. chili powder
½ tsp. cumin
1 tsp. ground cinnamon

DIRECTIONS:

1. Put nuts in slow cooker and pour melted butter over top. Toss to coat.

2. In small bowl, combine chili powder, cumin, and cinnamon. Sprinkle spice mixture over nuts and toss until well mixed.

3. Cover and cook on low for 2 to 2½ hours, stirring occasionally. Remove lid and cook on high for 10 to 15 minutes. Serve warm.

I like to set out a bowl of these nuts for snacking when I know that my guests will arrive before dinner's ready. They're also a great snack to keep on hand for long car rides or mid-afternoon munching.

Chicago Firehouse Chili

INGREDIENTS:

1 Tbsp. olive oil
1 large onion, chopped
2 cloves garlic, minced
1½ lbs. ground turkey
1 15-oz. can black beans, rinsed
    and drained
2 14.5-oz. cans diced tomatoes
    with chilies
1 15-oz. can and 1 10-oz. can
    pizza sauce
2 Tbsp. chili powder
1 tsp. cumin
1 Tbsp. Worcestershire sauce
1 tsp. freshly ground black pepper
½ lb. elbow macaroni, cooked according
    to package instructions (optional)
Toppings: shredded cheese, onions, tomatoes, sour cream

> This unusual chili recipe packs a punch of flavor! I like to serve this buffet style so the kids can choose their own toppings.

DIRECTIONS:

1. Heat oil in large skillet over medium heat. Add onion to pan and cook until soft, 5 to 8 minutes. Add garlic and cook 30 seconds. Transfer to slow cooker.

2. Brown turkey in same skillet. Transfer to slow cooker along with beans, diced tomatoes, pizza sauce, chili powder, cumin, Worcestershire sauce, and pepper. Stir well to combine.

3. Cover and cook on low for 7 to 8 hours, stirring occasionally. To serve, spoon over cooked macaroni and garnish with toppings.

Chicken Fajitas and Fixins'

INGREDIENTS:

1 tsp. chili powder
1 tsp. kosher salt
½ tsp. ground cumin
¼ tsp. garlic powder
1 Tbsp. cornstarch
½ cup water
3 Tbsp. olive oil
2 boneless, skinless chicken breasts, cut into ½-inch strips
1 green bell pepper, seeded and sliced
1 onion, thinly sliced
2 Tbsp. fresh lime juice, plus lime wedges for serving
12 flour tortillas, warmed in the slow cooker
Toppings: shredded lettuce, shredded cheddar cheese, salsa, sour cream, chopped tomatoes, guacamole

DIRECTIONS:

1. In small bowl, combine chili powder, salt, cumin, garlic, and cornstarch. Slowly mix in water and olive oil.

2. Lay chicken strips in bottom of slow cooker. Pour mixture over chicken and toss to coat. Add pepper and onion to slow cooker and squeeze lime juice over top.

3. Cover and cook on low for 3 hours. To serve, layer chicken, peppers, and onions into tortillas and add toppings of your choice.

Tortilla Warmer

INGREDIENTS:

Soft flour tortillas

DIRECTIONS:

1. Place tortillas in slow cooker. Sprinkle several drops of water over tortillas. Cover and cook on low for at least 15 minutes.

2. Serve on the warm setting.

No more cold and stiff tortillas! Keep them on the warm setting in the slow cooker, and they'll be ready when you want them.

Barbecue Meatballs and Southwestern Rice

Barbecue Meatballs

INGREDIENTS:

1 32-oz. package frozen meatballs
1 20-oz. can pineapple chunks
1 Tbsp. butter
1 onion, chopped
¾ cup ketchup
½ cup beef stock
3 Tbsp. Worcestershire sauce
1 Tbsp. white vinegar
½ cup brown sugar
3 Tbsp. lemon juice

DIRECTIONS:

1. Empty package of meatballs and can of pineapple into bottom of slow cooker.

2. Melt butter in skillet set over medium heat. Add onion and cook until softened, 5 to 8 minutes. Transfer to medium bowl, and add ketchup, beef stock, Worcestershire sauce, vinegar, brown sugar, and lemon juice. Whisk to combine.

3. Pour sauce over meatballs and pineapple and toss to coat. Cover and cook on low for 3 to 4 hours.

Southwestern Rice

INGREDIENTS:

2 cups brown rice
2 cups chicken broth
1½ cups water
1 Tbsp. butter
1 tsp. salt
1 tsp. cumin
1 4-oz. can chopped green chilies
1 cup corn
1 14.5-oz. can diced tomatoes
1 15-oz. can black beans, rinsed and drained
1 lime

DIRECTIONS:

1. Add rice, chicken broth, water, butter, salt, and cumin to greased slow cooker. Cover and cook on high for 1½ to 2 hours, stirring occasionally.

2. When little water remains, add chilies, corn, tomatoes, and black beans. Stir to combine.

3. Turn heat down to low, cover, and cook 1 additional hour. Squeeze lime juice over rice to serve.

Sunflower and Zucchini Avocado Toppings

Sunflower Topping

INGREDIENTS:

1½ cups sunflower seeds
¼ cup shredded coconut
½ cup pumpkin seeds
½ cup of almonds
½ cup soy nuts
1 Tbsp. coconut oil
2 tsp. apple pie spice
2 tsp. vanilla extract
¼ cup honey

DIRECTIONS:

1. Add all ingredients to greased slow cooker. Toss to combine.

2. Cover and cook on low for 1 hour.

Serve these delicious toppings over fresh avocado slices for a mouth-watering appetizer.

Zucchini Avocado Topping

INGREDIENTS:

1 cup fresh basil, roughly chopped
1 yellow bell pepper, diced
1 Tbsp. chili powder
2 tsp. fresh dill, finely chopped
2 cloves garlic, minced
Juice of 1 lemon, freshly squeezed
2 Tbsp. olive oil
1 bunch fresh cilantro leaves, chopped
3 zucchinis, chopped
2 tomatoes, diced
½ red onion, diced

DIRECTIONS:

1. Mix all ingredients in slow cooker. Toss gently to combine.

2. Cover and cook on low for 1 to 1½ hours.

This is also a great side dish with grilled fish.

Quick Whole Wheat Bread and Seafood Lasagna

Quick Whole Wheat Bread

INGREDIENTS:

- 2 cups whole wheat flour
- 1 cup all-purpose flour
- 2 tsp. baking soda
- 1 tsp. salt
- ¼ cup honey
- ¼ cup molasses
- 2 cups buttermilk

DIRECTIONS:

1. In a medium bowl, mix together flours, baking soda, and salt.

2. In a separate bowl, combine buttermilk, honey, and molasses. Add dry ingredients to buttermilk mixture and mix with rubber spatula until just combined.

3. Pour batter into greased rectangular bread pan. Set pan in slow cooker and cook on high for 1 to 1½ hours.

Seafood Lasagna

INGREDIENTS:

> 1 24-oz. jar alfredo sauce
> 1 24-oz. jar marinara sauce
> 10 wide no-boil lasagna noodles
> 1 cup fresh parmesan cheese, grated
> 2 Tbsp. olive oil
> 1 medium onion, sliced thin
> 2 tsp. salt
> 2 zucchini, peeled and julienned
> ½ lb. crabmeat, flaked
> ¼ lb. shrimp, peeled, cooked, and coarsely chopped
> 6 oz. fresh mozzarella, sliced ¼-inch thick
> 8 oz. ricotta cheese
> 3 egg whites, beaten

DIRECTIONS:

1. In large bowl, mix together olive oil, onion, salt, zucchini, crab, shrimp, mozzarella, ricotta, and egg whites.

2. Grease the slow cooker well and drizzle 1 cup of the marinara on the bottom. Lay 2 noodles on top, slightly overlapping. (Noodles will expand during cooking.)

3. Spread 1 cup of filling on top of noodles, then drizzle 1 cup alfredo sauce on top. Cover with 2 more lasagna noodles, slightly overlapping.

4. Use marinara sauce for second layer. Repeat layers until all sauce, filling, and noodles have been used up. End with sauce on top, then sprinkle with parmesan.

5. Cover and cook on low for 5 to 7 hours.

Mile-High Chicken Stacks and Baked Brie with Candied Walnuts & Cherries

Mile-High Chicken Stacks

INGREDIENTS:

2 lbs. boneless, skinless chicken breasts
1 lb. swiss cheese, thinly sliced
½ lb. green beans
18 marinated artichoke hearts, sliced
18 green olives, sliced
1 cup Italian dressing

DIRECTIONS:

1. Using a sharp knife, slice chicken breasts lengthwise to make wide, thin pieces. Lay ¼ of chicken in bottom of greased slow cooker. Top with ¼ of cheese, ¼ of green beans, ¼ of artichoke hearts, ¼ of green olives, and ¼ of Italian dressing.

2. Repeat layers three times. Cover and cook on low for 6 hours. Serve as a dip with whole grain pita chips.

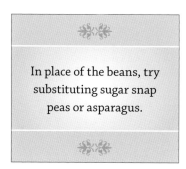

In place of the beans, try substituting sugar snap peas or asparagus.

Baked Brie with Candied Walnuts & Cherries

INGREDIENTS:

  1 small wheel of brie
  2 sheets phyllo dough, unthawed
  1 Tbsp. brown sugar
  1 Tbsp. water
  ½ tsp. balsamic vinegar
  ¼ tsp. dried rosemary or 1 tsp. chopped fresh rosemary
  ⅓ cup dried cherries, chopped
  ¼ cup walnuts, chopped

DIRECTIONS:

1. Take wrapper off brie. Lay cheese in center of phyllo sheets and wrap sheets up and around, pinching together at top.

2. Place small, oven-safe dish in slow cooker. Set wrapped brie inside dish.

3. In small bowl, combine brown sugar, water, vinegar, and rosemary. Stir in cherries and walnuts and pour over brie.

4. Cover and cook on low for 2 to 3 hours. Serve with crackers and apples slices.

Chicken Rice & Veggie Soup and Ski Country White Chili

Chicken Rice & Veggie Soup

INGREDIENTS:

8 cups chicken broth, preferably homemade
1 10-oz. can cream of mushroom soup
1 cup water
1 red bell pepper, chopped
1 carrot, peeled and chopped
1 stalk celery, chopped
1 small onion, chopped
2 cloves garlic, minced
¼ tsp. rosemary
1 tsp. freshly ground black pepper
½ cup uncooked rice
1 cup corn
1½ cups shredded cooked chicken

These soups are perfect to take to a church potluck!

DIRECTIONS:

1. Add broth, soup, and water to slow cooker and whisk to combine. Add bell pepper, carrot, celery, onion, garlic, rosemary, and pepper. Stir to combine. Cover and cook on low for 6 hours.

2. Add rice, corn, and shredded chicken to slow cooker. Cover and cook 2 additional hours.

Ski Country White Chili

INGREDIENTS:

1 Tbsp. olive oil
2 onions, chopped
2 lb. boneless, skinless chicken breasts, cooked and shredded
1 48-oz. jar Great Northern Beans, rinsed and drained
1 4-oz. can chopped green chilies
2 cloves garlic, minced
9 cups chicken stock, preferably homemade
1 Tbsp. cumin
Dash hot sauce
¼ tsp. cayenne pepper
¼ lb. havarti dill cheese

DIRECTIONS:

1. Heat oil in skillet set over medium heat until shimmering. Add onions and sauté until softened, 5 to 8 minutes. Transfer to slow cooker.

2. Add chicken, beans, chilies, garlic, chicken stock, cumin, hot sauce, and cayenne to slow cooker. Stir to mix well, then cover and cook on low for 6 to 7 hours.

3. Serve with havarti dill cheese and cornbread alongside.

This is our favorite white chili.
Don't despair if you have leftovers—
this is even better the second day!

Sweet and Savory Calas Toppings

Warm & Spicy Chocolate Sauce for Sweet Calas

INGREDIENTS:

2 lbs. chocolate bark
½ cup evaporated milk
½ cup brewed coffee
¼ cup honey
½ tsp. cinnamon
⅛ tsp. cayenne pepper
½ cup almonds, toasted

DIRECTIONS:

1. Break up chocolate bark and add to slow cooker. Pour in evaporated milk, coffee, honey, cinnamon, and cayenne. Cover and cook on low for 1 hour.

2. Once chocolate has melted, whisk sauce and add toasted almonds. Cover and cook 1 additional hour. Serve warm with sweet calas.

Calas are deep-fried rice cakes
traditional to Creole cuisine
in Louisiana. I usually spoon
this sauce over rice cakes for
a healthier alternative.

Warm Remoulade Sauce for Savory Calas

INGREDIENTS:

2 cups creole mustard
1 cup water
4 green onions, minced
½ cup parsley, minced
¼ cup olive oil
2 stalks celery, minced
4 Tbsp. paprika
½ tsp. cayenne
1 tsp. salt
Juice of 1 lemon

DIRECTIONS:

1. Add all ingredients to slow cooker and whisk to combine.

2. Cover and cook on low for 1 to 2 hours. Serve warm with savory calas.

Chapter 8

Vegetarian and Vegan

Invite to the banquet anyone you find.

Matthew 22:9

Tamale Pie

INGREDIENTS:

¾ cup yellow cornmeal
1½ cups milk
2 egg whites, beaten
1 8-oz. can black beans, rinsed and drained
1 Tbsp. chili powder
1 tsp. cumin
⅛ tsp. cayenne pepper
3 fresh tomatoes, chopped
1 16-oz. can whole kernel corn, drained
1 6-oz. can sliced ripe black olives, drained
Sour cream and guacamole, to serve

DIRECTIONS:

1. In a large bowl, whisk together cornmeal, milk, and egg whites. Add beans, chili powder, cumin, cayenne, tomatoes, corn, and olives. Toss gently to combine.

2. Transfer mixture to greased slow cooker. Cover and cook on low for 6 to 7 hours.

3. Cut into wedges and serve with sour cream and guacamole.

Molletes

INGREDIENTS:

- 1 24-oz. can pinto beans, rinsed and drained
- 2 Tbsp. extra virgin olive oil
- 1 clove garlic, minced
- 1 small onion, chopped
- 4 bolillos or other crusty roll, halved
- 1 cup shredded monterey jack cheese
- 1½ cups best quality fresh salsa

DIRECTIONS:

1. Add beans, olive oil, garlic, and onion to the slow cooker. Using a fork, mash the beans until they become spreadable, adding water 1 tsp. at a time, if needed. Cover and cook on low for 2 to 3 hours.

2. Preheat the oven broiler. Place the rolls on baking sheet and broil until golden, about 3 minutes. Spread each half of the rolls with about ½ cup of the bean mixture.

3. Top with shredded cheese and return to broiler until cheese is melted, 2 to 3 minutes. Serve with salsa.

Veggie Dogs with Steamed Buns and Homemade Ketchup

Veggie Dogs with Steamed Buns

INGREDIENTS:

1 package vegetarian hot dogs
¼ cup water
1 package whole grain hot dog rolls

DIRECTIONS:

1. Place veggie hot dogs and water in slow cooker. Cover and cook on low for 1 to 2 hours.

2. Place rolls in slow cooker on top of veggie hot dogs. Replace cover and steam for 5 minutes.

Homemade Ketchup

INGREDIENTS:

1 28-oz. can tomato puree
½ cup cider vinegar
⅔ cup brown sugar
1 Tbsp. olive oil
1 Tbsp. tomato paste
¼ tsp. dry mustard
½ tsp. kosher salt
¼ tsp. garlic powder
¼ tsp. onion powder
½ tsp. allspice
¼ tsp. smoked paprika

DIRECTIONS:

1. Pour all ingredients in greased slow cooker. Cover and cook on low, stirring occasionally, for 3 hours, or until thickened to desired consistency.

2. Let cool before serving. Store in an airtight container in the fridge.

My kids like homemade ketchup better than the bottled stuff! They put it on everything from hamburgers to scrambled eggs!

Pumpkin Pies in a Jar

INGREDIENTS:

4 egg whites, beaten
1½ cups brown sugar, packed
1 tsp. salt
1 tsp. ground cinnamon
1½ tsp. pumpkin pie spice
2 cups canned pumpkin
1 12-oz. can fat free evaporated milk
1 cup graham cracker crumbs
1 cup whipping cream
1 tsp. vanilla
2 tsp. sugar
4 6- or 8-oz. glass canning jars

This is Thanksgiving in a jar— all year long!

DIRECTIONS:

1. Coat inside of jars with nonstick cooking spray. Set aside.

2. In large bowl, combine egg whites and brown sugar. Stir in salt, cinnamon, and pie spice. Gradually whisk in evaporated milk, then stir in pumpkin. Whisk until smooth.

3. Pour filling into jars and set filled jars in slow cooker. Cover and cook on low for 3 to 5 hours. Remove jars from slow cooker and let cool at least 10 minutes.

4. Combine whipping cream, vanilla, and sugar in large bowl. Beat with electric beaters until stiff peaks form.

5. To serve, sprinkle graham cracker crumbs on each jar of pumpkin. Top with whipped cream.

Sweet Potatoes au Gratin

INGREDIENTS:

4 sweet potatoes, peeled and sliced into ¼-inch rounds
2 Tbsp. orange juice, freshly squeezed
2 tsp. orange zest
2 Tbsp. butter, melted
¼ cup dark brown sugar
2 Tbsp. cream
½ tsp. cinnamon
½ tsp. salt
¾ cup crumbled goat cheese
½ cup plain bread crumbs, toasted

DIRECTIONS:

1. Layer sweet potato slices in bottom of greased slow cooker.

2. Combine all remaining ingredients in small bowl. Pour over potatoes.

3. Cover and cook on high for 3 to 4 hours.

4. Sprinkle crumbled goat cheese and breadcrumbs over potatoes just before serving.

My family loves the melting sweetness of these potatoes. The hint of orange is my secret ingredient!

Soy & Ginger Fondue and Mocha Fondue

Soy & Ginger Fondue

INGREDIENTS:

4 cups vegetable stock
¼ cup soy sauce
4 tsp. fresh ginger root, minced
1 clove garlic, minced
¼ cup honey
¼ cup orange juice, freshly squeezed
1 bay leaf
To serve: Baby carrots, cauliflower, broccoli, celery, asparagus, cubed tofu

DIRECTIONS:

1. In slow cooker, whisk together vegetable stock, soy sauce, ginger, garlic, honey, and orange juice. Add bay leaf. Cover and cook on high for 2 hours.

2. Pour liquid into fondue pot if available, or dip veggies directly into slow cooker.

Mocha Fondue

INGREDIENTS:

1 lb. semisweet chocolate, chopped
1 cup evaporated milk
¼ cup espresso
1 tsp. vanilla
To serve: strawberries, bananas, oreos, raspberries, cubed
   angel food cake, marshmallows

DIRECTIONS:

1. Combine chocolate, evaporated milk, and espresso in slow
   cooker. Cover and cook on low for three hours, stirring
   occasionally.

2. Stir in vanilla just before serving. Pour chocolate into
   fondue pot, if available, or serve directly in slow cooker.

This is the ultimate
chocolate fondue. If you
have leftovers, serve it
over ice cream tomorrow!

Ranch Mushrooms and Hawaiian Rice

Ranch Mushrooms

INGREDIENTS:

- 5 16-oz. packages whole mushrooms
- ¼ cup extra virgin olive oil
- ¼ tsp. salt
- ¼ tsp. garlic powder
- 1 tsp. onion powder
- ¼ tsp. freshly ground black pepper
- ¼ tsp. sugar
- ½ tsp. paprika
- ½ tsp. dried parsley

DIRECTIONS:

1. Place mushrooms in slow cooker.

2. In separate bowl, combine salt, garlic powder, onion powder, pepper, sugar, paprika, and parsley. Add olive oil and stir to combine. Pour over mushrooms and toss gently to coat.

3. Cover and cook on low for 3 to 4 hours.

This entrée is also a delicious side dish to serve with grilled steak.

Hawaiian Rice

INGREDIENTS:

- 2 cups dry rice
- 4 cups water
- ½ tsp. salt
- 1 cup crushed pineapple
- 1 cup sliced almonds or crushed macadamia nuts
- ½ tsp. allspice

DIRECTIONS:

1. Pour rice, water, and salt into greased slow cooker. Cover and cook on low for 2 to 2½ hours.

2. Fluff with a fork and stir in pineapple, nuts, and allspice.

Hot Potato Salad and Avocado Mushroom Burgers

Hot Potato Salad

INGREDIENTS:

1 cup mayonnaise
2 tsp. lemon juice, freshly squeezed
½ tsp. salt
6 red bliss potatoes, cut into ½-inch cubes
1 cup chopped celery
1 cup chopped walnuts

DIRECTIONS:

1. Mix together mayonnaise, lemon juice, and salt in small bowl. Set aside.

2. Put potatoes, celery, and walnuts in greased slow cooker. Pour mayonnaise over top and toss gently to coat.

3. Cover and cook on low for 3 to 4 hours.

This is a basic recipe, but change it up according to your tastes, your favorite spices, and the contents of your vegetable crisper! It's delicious with green beans, raisins, dry mustard, and tarragon.

Avocado Mushroom Burgers

INGREDIENTS:

4 portabella mushrooms, stems
    removed
1 onion, sliced thin
3 Tbsp. olive oil
1 tsp. salt, divided
1 tsp. freshly ground black pepper,
    divided
2 tsp. Worcestershire sauce
1 avocado, sliced
1 Tbsp. plain yogurt
½ tsp. garlic powder
1 tsp. lemon juice
4 whole wheat hamburger rolls,
    lightly toasted

This is my go-to dish when I need a vegetarian alternative at a casual evening gathering. But even the meat-eaters will pass up a burger for a taste of these.

DIRECTIONS:

1. Place mushrooms in greased slow cooker. Brush with oil and scatter onion slices over top. Sprinkle with Worcestershire sauce and ½ tsp. each salt and pepper. Cover and cook on low for 2 hours, turning occasionally.

2. Meanwhile, in a small bowl combine half the avocado, yogurt, garlic powder, and remaining ½ tsp. each salt and pepper. Mash until smooth. Sprinkle with lemon juice and set aside.

3. Spoon onions into mushroom cavities. Spread smooth avocado mixture on bottom of each roll and place stuffed mushrooms on top. Top mushrooms with remaining sliced avocado and cover with second half of roll.

Carolina Taco Soup and Queso Dip

Carolina Taco Soup

INGREDIENTS:

1 14.5-oz. can diced tomatoes, undrained
2 cups best quality fresh salsa
1 14.5-oz. can tomato sauce
1 qt. vegetable stock
2 15-oz. cans pinto beans, rinsed and drained
2 cups corn
1 Tbsp. cumin
¼ tsp. cayenne pepper
½ tsp. freshly ground black pepper
1 tsp. dried oregano
Tortilla chips
1 cup shredded cheddar cheese
2 cups lettuce, shredded

DIRECTIONS:

1. Combine diced tomatoes, salsa, tomato sauce, vegetable stock, beans, corn, cumin, cayenne, pepper, and oregano in slow cooker. Cover and cook on low for 6 to 8 hours.

2. Ladle into bowls, and top each serving with shredded lettuce and cheddar. Serve with tortilla chips.

If you have time, make this soup a day in advance to give the flavors time to meld.

Queso Dip

INGREDIENTS:

2 lb. processed cheese, cubed
2 large tomatoes, diced
1 4-oz. can diced green chilies
1 Tbsp. Worcestershire sauce
1 tsp. freshly ground black pepper
1 tsp. onion powder
1 tsp. garlic powder
Tortilla or corn chips

DIRECTIONS:

1. Combine cheese, tomatoes, chilies, Worcestershire sauce, pepper, onion powder, and garlic powder in slow cooker. Stir to combine.

2. Cover and cook on low for 2 to 3 hours, stirring occasionally, until cheese is fully melted.

3. Turn to warm setting and serve with tortilla chips.

Sweet Rye Bread
and Tofu Mostaccioli

Sweet Rye Bread

INGREDIENTS:

Nonstick spray
2 cups rye flour
½ cup all-purpose flour
2 tsp. salt
1 tsp. baking powder
½ tsp. baking soda
⅓ cup untoasted sunflower seeds, optional
2 Tbsp. flaxseed, optional
1 Tbsp. olive oil
1 cup plain yogurt
¼ cup whole milk
¼ cup honey or brown sugar
2 egg whites, beaten
2 Tbsp. sesame seeds, for garnish

DIRECTIONS:

1. Grease and lightly flour a bread pan. In a large bowl, mix together flours, salt, baking powder, baking soda, and seeds.

2. In a second bowl, whisk together olive oil, yogurt, milk, honey, and eggs. Pour into flour mixture and stir well to combine.

3. Pour batter into prepared bread pan and sprinkle sesame seeds on top of dough. Place bread pan in slow cooker. Cover and cook on high for 1½ to 2 hours, checking frequently.

4. Let cool in pan for 10 minutes, then turn out onto wire rack.

Tofu Mostaccioli

INGREDIENTS:

1 12-oz. package of silken tofu, diced
½ cup Italian dressing
3 large tomatoes, chopped
5 fresh basil leaves, chopped
1 16-oz. package mostaccoli, uncooked
2 cups water
½ cup balsamic vinaigrette dressing
8 oz. mozzarella cheese, grated and divided
¼ cup parmesan, freshly grated

DIRECTIONS:

1. Marinate tofu in Italian dressing for one hour.

2. Mix mostaccioli, water, tomatoes, basil leaves, balsamic vinaigrette dressing, marinated tofu, and half the mozzarella in slow cooker. Cover and cook on low for 2 to 3 hours.

3. Top with remaining mozzarella and parmesan. Cover and cook on low for 30 additional minutes.

This pasta dish is as much a staple in our house as spaghetti and meatballs.

Royal Pumpkin Lasagna

INGREDIENTS:

1 4- to 5-lb. baking pumpkin
1 tsp. paprika
1 tsp. fresh nutmeg, freshly grated
1 tsp. freshly ground black pepper
1 tsp. salt
1 cup fresh ricotta cheese
2 egg whites, beaten
2 Tbsp. Italian seasoning
8 to 10 sheets no-boil lasagna noodles
⅔ cup milk
1 cup alfredo sauce
1 cup water
4 oz. grated parmesan cheese

This rich, colorful lasagna signals the start of fall in our household. If you're pressed for time you can also use canned pumpkin puree.

DIRECTIONS:

1. Preheat oven to 275°. Set pumpkin on baking sheet and cook until tender, 50 to 60 minutes. Scoop the flesh off the rind, reserving seeds, and place in medium bowl.

2. Season the pumpkin with paprika, nutmeg, pepper, and salt. Mash with a potato masher.

3. In a separate bowl, mix the ricotta cheese, egg whites, and Italian seasoning.

4. Grease slow cooker and arrange a layer of lasagna noodles in the bottom. Spoon ⅓ of the pumpkin mixture on top.

5. Lay noodles over the top, followed by another layer of pumpkin and another noodle layer.

6. Add a layer with all the ricotta cheese mixture, followed by another layer of pasta.

7. Add remaining pumpkin mixture, followed by a final layer of noodles.

8. In small bowl, mix alfredo sauce, milk, and water. Pour over top of lasagna and allow it to drain through to all pasta layers. Cover and cook on low for 4 to 5 hours.

9. Sprinkle with grated parmesan. Cover and cook 1 additional hour.

Pumpkin Seeds

INGREDIENTS:

Pumpkin seeds, reserved from Royal Pumpkin Lasagna
1 Tbsp. butter, melted
1 tsp. sea salt

DIRECTIONS:

1. Preheat oven to 250°. Rinse seeds, using fingers to remove all the pulp. Drain well, discarding pulp. Spread seeds out on a rimmed baking sheet and bake about 15 minutes, or until dry.

2. Line bottom of slow cooker with aluminum foil. Add seeds, butter, and salt to slow cooker and toss gently to coat.

3. Cover and cook on high for 45 minutes, stirring occasionally. Use to garnish Royal Pumpkin Lasagna or for snacking.

Pad Thai and Tangy Peanut Soup

Pad Thai

INGREDIENTS:

1 lb. firm tofu, cut into ½-inch pieces
8 oz. mushrooms, sliced
1 red bell pepper, seeded and chopped
1 yellow bell pepper, seeded and chopped
8 oz. snow peas
1 cup bean sprouts
¼ cup crushed peanuts
½ cup creamy peanut butter
2 Tbsp. lime juice, freshly squeezed
¼ cup coconut milk
1 Tbsp. soy sauce
1 tsp. grated fresh ginger
2 cloves garlic, minced
1 tsp. crushed red pepper flakes
1 lb. rice noodles, cooked
1 lime, sliced

DIRECTIONS:

1. Put tofu, mushrooms, peppers, snow peas, bean sprouts, and peanuts in slow cooker.

2. In separate bowl, whisk together peanut butter, lime juice, coconut milk, soy sauce, ginger, garlic, and red pepper flakes. Pour over contents of slow cooker, tossing gently to combine.

3. Cover and cook on low for 3 to 4 hours. Serve over rice noodles and garnish with lime.

Tangy Peanut Soup

INGREDIENTS:

2 onions, sliced
2 cloves garlic, minced
2 sweet potatoes, peeled and cut into chunks
1 28-oz. can diced tomatoes
6 cups vegetable stock
½ cup chunky peanut butter
1 Tbsp. curry powder
1 tsp. salt
1 tsp. freshly ground black
   pepper
¼ tsp. cayenne pepper
1 cup coconut milk
2 Tbsp. crushed peanuts
6 sprigs cilantro

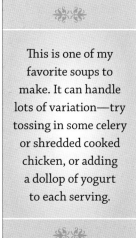

This is one of my favorite soups to make. It can handle lots of variation—try tossing in some celery or shredded cooked chicken, or adding a dollop of yogurt to each serving.

DIRECTIONS:

1. Add the onion, garlic, sweet potatoes, and tomatoes to slow cooker. In separate bowl, whisk together vegetable stock, peanut butter, curry, salt, pepper, and cayenne. Pour mixture over vegetables.

2. Cover and cook on low for 6 hours. Stir in coconut milk, cover, and cook 1 additional hour. Ladle into bowls and garnish with a few crushed peanuts and a sprig of cilantro to serve.

Homemade Strawberry Jam and Pipin' Hot Bread with Sea Salt

Homemade Strawberry Jam

INGREDIENTS:

2 pints strawberries, washed and hulled
2½ cups white grape juice (divided)
1 packet of sugar-free pectin
Peanut butter or almond butter, to use on sandwiches

DIRECTIONS:

1. Mash strawberries by hand in large bowl. Pour into slow cooker and stir in 2 cups white grape juice. Cover and cook on low for 2 to 4 hours, stirring occasionally.

2. In separate bowl, whisk pectin into ½ cup cold juice. Pour mixture into slow cooker and stir to combine. Cover and cook an additional 30 to 60 minutes.

3. Ladle the jam into the freezer containers, leaving at least ½ inch of space at the top. Cover and store in freezer.

Pipin' Hot Bread with Sea Salt

INGREDIENTS:

1 frozen bread loaf from your grocery store freezer section
2 Tbsp. olive oil
2 tsp. sea salt

DIRECTIONS:

1. Rub olive oil all over frozen loaf. Place loaf in bottom of slow cooker and sprinkle with sea salt.

2. Cover and cook on low for 2 to 2½ hours, checking frequently to prevent burning. Serve plain or with strawberry jam and peanut butter.

Spaghetti Squash Tacos and Black Beans & Rice

Spaghetti Squash Tacos

INGREDIENTS:

- 1 large spaghetti squash, halved and seeded
- 2 tsp. olive oil
- 2 tsp. cumin
- ¼ tsp. cayenne
- ½ tsp. oregano
- ½ tsp. salt
- 1 onion, chopped
- 1 jalapeno pepper, seeded and diced
- 12 crisp taco shells
- 1 cup guacamole, to serve

Instead of guacamole, try topping the tacos with diced tomatoes, shredded lettuce, and sour cream.

DIRECTIONS:

1. Grease inside of slow cooker. Place the two halves of the squash inside, with the cut sides facing.

2. In a separate bowl, whisk together olive oil, cumin, cayenne, oregano, salt, onion, and jalapeno pepper. Pour over and around squash. Cover and cook on low for 4 hours.

3. Remove the spaghetti squash from the slow cooker and scoop out flesh. Shred squash with a fork and return to slow cooker, discarding skin.

4. Stuff into taco shells to serve. Top with guacamole.

Black Beans & Rice

INGREDIENTS:

   1 tsp. olive oil
   1½ cups uncooked white rice
   3 cups vegetable stock
   1 tsp. ground cumin
   ¼ tsp. cayenne pepper
   3½ cups canned black beans, rinsed and drained
   1 cup salsa, to serve

DIRECTIONS:

1. Add oil, rice, vegetable stock, cumin, and cayenne to slow cooker. Mix well. Cover and cook on low for 1½ hours.

2. Add the black beans and cook 1 hour longer. Serve with salsa.

Chapter 9

Without the Cow: Dairy Free

*Then you and your household shall eat there in
the presence of the LORD your God and rejoice.*

DEUTERONOMY 14:26

Carrot Top Couscous Soup and Pineapple Upside-Down Cake

Carrot Top Couscous Soup

INGREDIENTS:

2 shallots, minced

8 cups beef stock

4 carrots, peeled and cut into ¼-inch rounds

1 cup fresh carrot tops, washed and finely chopped

¾ cup couscous, cooked according to package instructions

1 tsp. salt

1 tsp. freshly ground black pepper

DIRECTIONS:

1. Add the shallots, beef stock, carrots, and carrot tops to the slow cooker. Cover and cook on low for 6 to 8 hours.

2. Just before serving stir in couscous, salt, and pepper.

Carrot greens are delicious and packed full of vitamins. It's a shame they aren't used more, but this recipe will make you a convert!

Pineapple Upside-Down Cake

INGREDIENTS:

6 Tbsp. margarine
1 cup brown sugar, divided
6 to 8 pineapple rings
1 20-oz can crushed pineapple, drained, juice reserved
8 maraschino cherries
¼ cup pineapple juice (reserved from can)

¾ cup flour
¾ cup sugar
1 tsp. baking powder
½ tsp. cinnamon
½ tsp. nutmeg
¼ tsp. salt
2 eggs
2 Tbsp. milk

DIRECTIONS:

1. Make an aluminum foil sling by lining the inside of the slow cooker with foil. Foil should go at least six inches up the sides of the slow cooker. Grease foil well.

2. Melt margarine and pour in slow cooker. Sprinkle brown sugar evenly over butter. Arrange pineapple rings in bottom of slow cooker without overlapping. (You may have to cut some in half in order to cover the whole bottom.) Place cherries in the center of each pineapple ring.

3. Spoon the drained crushed pineapple over the rings, patting even with rubber spatula.

4. In large bowl, combine the flour, sugar, baking powder, cinnamon, nutmeg, and salt. In separate bowl, whisk together the eggs, milk, and reserved pineapple juice. Add to the flour mixture and beat well to combine.

5. Pour the batter over the crushed pineapple. Cover and cook on high for 1½ to 2 hours. Remove cake with foil sling and let cool before serving.

Rhubarb Punch and Spicy Walnuts

Rhubarb Punch

INGREDIENTS:

6 cups finely chopped rhubarb
⅓ cup sugar
¼ cup orange juice concentrate
3 qt. water

DIRECTIONS:

1. Combine rhubarb, sugar, orange juice concentrate, and water in slow cooker. Cover and cook on low for 8 to 10 hours. Strain through fine-mesh strainer, discarding solids.

2. To serve hot, ladle punch into mugs. To serve cold, let punch sit at room temperature for 1 hour, then cover and refrigerate up to 4 days.

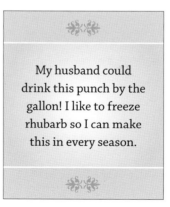

My husband could drink this punch by the gallon! I like to freeze rhubarb so I can make this in every season.

Spicy Walnuts

INGREDIENTS:

2 Tbsp. melted butter
1 tsp. ground cinnamon
1 tsp. ground nutmeg
1 tsp. ground cloves
4 cups walnuts
1 cup raisins
1 cup golden raisins

DIRECTIONS:

1. Add melted butter, cinnamon, nutmeg, cloves, and walnuts to slow cooker. Toss to combine. Cover and cook on low for 2 to 4 hours.

2. Add raisins just before serving.

Blackened Salmon

INGREDIENTS:

2 tsp. dry mustard
½ tsp. cayenne pepper
1 tsp. ground cumin
1½ tsp. black pepper
1 tsp. white pepper
1 tsp. dried thyme
1 tsp. salt
1 tsp. paprika
6 4-oz. salmon fillets
2 Tbsp. olive oil

The spice mixture on this salmon is simply unbeatable. I've used the same mix as a substitute for taco seasoning packets and even in macaroni and cheese!

DIRECTIONS:

1. Mix together dry mustard, cayenne, cumin, black pepper, white pepper, thyme, salt, and paprika. Set aside.

2. Grease inside of slow cooker and arrange fillets inside. Brush each fillet with olive oil and sprinkle spice mixture over top, pressing in with fingers.

3. Cover and cook on high for 1 hour.

Black-Eyed Peas & Okra

INGREDIENTS:

32 oz. frozen black-eyed peas
2 cups water
1 onion, chopped
1 green pepper, seeded and chopped
2 stalks celery, chopped
16 oz. frozen okra
1 14.5-oz. can diced tomatoes with green chilies

DIRECTIONS:

1. Put all ingredients in slow cooker, stirring well to combine.

2. Cover and cook on low for 8 to 9 hours.

Try this veggie side dish spooned over rice or couscous.

Lemon Tea Soup
and Secret Baked Bananas

Lemon Tea Soup

INGREDIENTS:

1 clove garlic, minced
½ onion, chopped
1 cup carrots, chopped
1 apple, peeled and chopped
1 stalk celery, chopped
8 cups water
1 bay leaf
⅛ tsp. freshly ground black pepper
½ cup iced tea powder with lemon
¾ cup polenta
1 Tbsp. parsley, chopped

DIRECTIONS:

1. Combine garlic, onion, carrots, apple, celery, water, bay leaf, and pepper in slow cooker. Mix well. Cover and cook on low for 6 to 8 hours.

2. Add polenta. Cover and cook an additional 20 minutes. Discard bay leaf; stir in iced tea powder and chopped parsley.

I like to garnish this soup by floating a slice of lemon in each bowl.

Secret Baked Bananas

INGREDIENTS:

6 whole bananas
Miniature marshmallows
Peanut butter
Chocolate chips
Peanut butter chips
Butterscotch chips
Blueberries
Raspberries
Peanuts

I love making this dish with children and letting them choose their own fillings. But be prepared for some cleanup after they finish eating!

DIRECTIONS:

1. Slice banana down the middle, being careful to not slice all the way through. Carefully cut away a wedge section of the peel and discard.

2. Pinch the banana inward to open up the banana. Fill with chocolate, candy, marshmallows, or berries. Wrap each banana in aluminum foil and place in greased slow cooker.

3. Cover and cook on low 2 hours. To serve, open the aluminum foil and sprinkle banana with peanuts.

South of the Border Caramel Baked Apples

INGREDIENTS:

4 apples
½ cup apple juice
½ cup brown sugar
¼ tsp. cloves
¼ tsp. anise
¾ tsp. cinnamon
4 caramels (optional)

DIRECTIONS:

1. Peel ¾ inch off top of each apple. Core each apple partway through, leaving about ½-inch portion from the bottom intact.

2. In a small bowl, mix the brown sugar, cloves, anise, and cinnamon. Fill the center of each apple with the brown sugar mixture, and press a caramel into the top, if desired.

3. Pour the apple juice in the bottom of the slow cooker, then place the apples in the pot. Cover and cook on low for 3 to 5 hours, or until apples are tender.

Easy Bean Burritos

INGREDIENTS:

1 onion, quartered
3 cups dry pinto beans, rinsed and picked over
1 4-oz. can chopped green chilies
2 cloves garlic, minced
2 tsp. salt
1 tsp. cumin
2 qts. water
1 red onion, sliced
2 tomatoes, sliced
1 zucchini, sliced
1 cucumber, sliced
1 green bell pepper, seeded and
   sliced
1 tsp. freshly ground black pepper
8 7-inch flour tortillas

The bean mixture in this recipe surpasses anything you'll find in a can. Top the burritos with any veggies you like. I also like to use spinach and feta cheese!

DIRECTIONS:

1. Combine onion, beans, chilies, garlic, salt, cumin, and water in slow cooker, stirring well to combine. Cover and cook on high for 8 hours, adding water if necessary.

2. Drain beans, reserving liquid. Mash with a potato masher, adding reserved cooking liquid until smooth.

3. Spread beans over tortillas and top with red onion, tomato, zucchini, cucumber, and bell peppers. Grind pepper over top of veggies and roll up tortilla to serve.

Grapefruit-Mango Fish and Basil Couscous

Grapefruit-Mango Fish

INGREDIENTS:

6 whitefish fillets
1 Tbsp. olive oil
1 ruby red grapefruit
2 mangos, sliced
1 red onion, sliced
1 tsp. salt
½ tsp. pepper
1 Tbsp. vinegar
1½ cups white grape juice

DIRECTIONS:

1. Heat oil in skillet over medium heat until shimmering. Add fish and brown, 5 to 8 minutes per side. Transfer to slow cooker.

2. Add grapefruit sections, mangoes, red onion, salt, pepper, vinegar, and white grape juice to slow cooker. Cover and cook on low for 4 to 6 hours. Serve over basil couscous.

As a variation, add a handful of kumquats to the slow cooker. You'll love the burst of citrus flavor!

Basil Couscous

INGREDIENTS:

2 cups couscous
4½ cups water
2 tsp. olive oil
1 tsp. salt
¼ cup fresh basil, chopped

DIRECTIONS:

1. Combine couscous, water, olive oil, and salt in slow cooker. Cover and cook for 30 minutes on low.

2. Fluff with fork and toss with chopped basil leaves.

Hungarian Goulash and Stuffed Mushrooms

Hungarian Goulash

INGREDIENTS:

2 lbs. beef, cubed
1 Tbsp. olive oil
1½ cups chopped onion
1 tsp. salt
2 Tbsp. brown sugar
1 Tbsp. paprika
½ tsp. dry mustard
2 Tbsp. Worcestershire sauce
1 cup tomato sauce
1¼ cups water, divided
¼ cup flour
16 oz. cooked egg noodles

You won't believe the aroma in the house after this has been cooking all day!

DIRECTIONS:

1. Heat oil in skillet set over medium heat until shimmering. Brown meat in olive oil, then transfer to slow cooker. Add onion.

2. In separate bowl, whisk together salt, brown sugar, paprika, and dry mustard. Slowly whisk in Worcestershire sauce, tomato sauce, and 1 cup water. Pour sauce over meat and onions. Cover and cook on low for 8 to 10 hours, or until beef is tender.

3. Using a fork, mix together flour and remaining ¼ cup water in small bowl. Add mixture to goulash and stir to combine. Cover and cook 15 to 20 additional minutes to thicken.

4. Serve over egg noodles.

CREATIVE SLOW-COOKER MEALS ⁓ *Without the Cow: Dairy Free*

Stuffed Mushrooms

INGREDIENTS:

18 button mushrooms, stems separated from caps
2 Tbsp. olive oil, divided
2 shallots, minced
1 clove garlic, minced
2 Tbsp. chopped walnuts
1 tsp. salt
2 Tbsp. parsley, chopped
1 tsp. dried thyme
2 Tbsp. plain breadcrumbs
2 Tbsp. chicken stock
2 Tbsp. olive oil

DIRECTIONS:

1. Finely chop the mushroom stems. Transfer to a medium bowl and add 1 Tbsp. olive oil, shallots, garlic, walnuts, and salt. Mix well, then stir in parsley, thyme, and breadcrumbs.

2. Transfer mixture to food processor. Pulse several times until mixture is almost smooth.

3. In separate bowl, toss mushroom caps with chicken stock and remaining Tbsp. olive oil. Fill each mushroom with the stuffing. Set stuffed mushrooms right side up in slow cooker. Cover and cook on low for 3 to 4 hours.

Maple Meatballs and Orange-Cranberry Sauce

Maple Meatballs

INGREDIENTS:

- 1 lb. ground turkey
- ¾ teaspoon salt
- ½ tsp. dried sage
- ½ tsp. freshly ground pepper
- ¼ tsp. ground ginger
- 2 egg whites, beaten
- 1 8-oz. can crushed pineapple, drained, juice reserved
- 1 cup real maple syrup
- 1 cup ketchup
- 2 Tbsp. soy sauce

These meatballs are delicious on any occasion—graduation parties, family gatherings, and Sunday brunch!

DIRECTIONS:

1. Preheat oven to 350°.

2. In a large bowl, mix together ground turkey, salt, sage, pepper, ginger, egg whites, and crushed pineapple. Form mixture into 1-inch balls and place on parchment-lined baking sheets. Place in oven and bake until browned, 20 to 25 minutes.

3. Place baked meatballs into slow cooker. In a separate bowl, mix drained pineapple juice, maple syrup, ketchup, and soy sauce. Pour mixture over the meatballs. Cover and cook on low for 2 to 3 hours.

Orange-Cranberry Sauce

INGREDIENTS:

12 oz. fresh or frozen cranberries
1 orange, sliced into sections
¾ cup freshly squeezed orange juice
½ cup water
½ cup brown sugar
½ cup white sugar
¼ tsp. cinnamon
¼ tsp. nutmeg
¼ tsp. cloves

DIRECTIONS:

1. Combine all ingredients in slow cooker. Cover and cook on high for 3 hours, stirring once every hour. Mash cranberries as the skin softens.

2. Remove lid and continue cooking on high for 45 minutes, stirring occasionally. Serve with maple meatballs.

Eggplant Boats
and Chicken in a Pot

Eggplant Boats

INGREDIENTS:

1 eggplant
1 Tbsp. olive oil
1 Tbsp. onion flakes
1 tsp. garlic powder
2 egg whites, beaten
1 cup bread crumbs, divided

DIRECTIONS:

1. Cut eggplant in half lengthwise and scoop out flesh with a spoon, reserving skin. Heat oil in saucepan set over medium heat until shimmering. Add eggplant and cook until tender.

2. Transfer cooked eggplant to medium bowl and combine with onion flakes, garlic powder, egg whites, and ½ cup bread crumbs. Mix well. Stuff eggplant skins with mixture and lay in greased slow cooker. Sprinkle remaining ½ cup bread crumbs over top and dot with olive oil.

3. Cover and cook on high for 2 to 3 hours. To serve, cut each eggplant half into 2 or 3 pieces.

Chicken in a Pot

INGREDIENTS:

3 lbs. chicken thighs, skin on
¼ cup olive oil
1 tsp. salt
1 tsp. freshly ground black pepper
3 carrots, peeled
2 tsp. chopped fresh rosemary
2 cloves garlic, minced
2 tsp. chopped fresh thyme
3 red bliss potatoes, quartered
1 bulb fennel, cut in wedges
1 bulb celery root, cut in wedges
2 cups chicken stock
1 lemon

DIRECTIONS:

1. Heat oil until shimmering in Dutch oven set over medium heat. Season chicken thighs with salt and pepper, then put in Dutch oven and brown, 5 to 7 minutes per side. Transfer chicken to slow cooker along with any juices.

This is a classic Sunday dinner recipe. I like to start it as soon as we get home from church, and then rest easy during the afternoon.

2. Add carrots, rosemary, garlic, thyme, potatoes, fennel, celery root, and chicken stock to slow cooker. Squeeze lemon over chicken. Cover and cook on low for 6 to 7 hours.

Balsamic-Braised Chicken with Olives and Spiced Applesauce

Balsamic-Braised Chicken with Olives

INGREDIENTS:

1 Tbsp. olive oil
3½ lbs. chicken pieces
2 onions, chopped
4 cloves garlic, minced
1 tsp. salt
½ tsp. cracked black peppercorns
½ tsp. dried thyme leaves
1 14.5-oz. can diced tomatoes
1 cup chicken stock
2 Tbsp. balsamic vinegar
1 6-oz. can marinated artichoke hearts
2 Tbsp. chopped black olives
2 Tbsp. capers

DIRECTIONS:

1. Heat olive oil in skillet set over medium heat. Add chicken, in batches, and brown on all sides.

2. Transfer chicken to slow cooker, stirring in any juices from skillet. Add all remaining ingredients. Cover and cook on low for 7 to 8 hours.

Spiced Applesauce

INGREDIENTS:

4 lbs. Macintosh apples
4 lbs. Jonathan apples
1 tsp. lemon juice
½ tsp. cinnamon
1 Tbsp. brown sugar
¼ cup water

DIRECTIONS:

1. Skin, core, and quarter apples. Transfer apples to slow cooker. Sprinkle with lemon juice, cinnamon, brown sugar, and water.

2. Cover and cook on low for 4 to 6 hours.

3. When apples are very tender, mash with potato masher. Transfer to large serving bowl. Let cool and sprinkle with a pinch of cinnamon.

For a variation, try mashing fresh berries into the sauce.

Creamy Tomato Basil Soup and Garlic Broccoli & Cauliflower

Creamy Tomato Basil Soup

INGREDIENTS:

2 28-oz. cans crushed tomatoes
4 cups water or chicken stock
1 tsp. salt
2 cloves garlic, minced
½ cup fresh basil, chopped
½ cup soy milk

DIRECTIONS:

1. Stir together the crushed tomatoes, water or chicken stock, salt, garlic, and basil in slow cooker.

2. Cover and cook on low for 4 to 6 hours.

3. Stir in soy milk. Cover and cook on low for 20 additional minutes, or until heated through.

Garnish this soup
with garlic croutons
and julienned basil.
Beats anything
you'll find in a can!

Garlic Broccoli & Cauliflower

INGREDIENTS:

2 lbs. broccoli
1 lb. cauliflower
3 Tbsp. extra virgin olive oil
2 Tbsp. water
6 cloves garlic, minced
½ tsp. salt
¼ tsp. cayenne pepper

DIRECTIONS:

1. Chop broccoli and cauliflower into florets. Transfer to greased slow cooker along with all remaining ingredients. Toss gently to coat.

2. Cover and cook on low for 5 to 6 hours, stirring several times.

This is also delicious garnished with chopped cashews.

Honey Roasted Chicken and Chunky Triple Fruit Sauce

Honey Roasted Chicken

INGREDIENTS:

- 1 3- to 4-lb. whole chicken
- 1 tsp. salt
- 2 tsp. freshly ground black pepper
- ¼ cup honey
- 2 Tbsp. Dijon mustard

DIRECTIONS:

1. Place chicken in greased slow cooker.

2. In separate bowl, whisk together salt, pepper, honey, and mustard. Pour over chicken, spreading with a spatula to cover top. Cover and cook on low for 5 to 7 hours, or until internal temperature reaches 160°. Remove from slow cooker and let rest 10 minutes before carving.

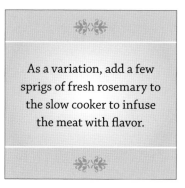

As a variation, add a few sprigs of fresh rosemary to the slow cooker to infuse the meat with flavor.

Chunky Triple Fruit Sauce

INGREDIENTS:

5 apples, peeled and cored
5 pears, peeled and cored
5 peaches, peeled and cored
½ cup water
1 Tbsp. cinnamon

DIRECTIONS:

1. Place apples, pears, and peaches in slow cooker. Pour water over top. Cover and cook on low for 6 to 7 hours.

2. When fruit is tender, mash with a fork or potato masher. Sprinkle with cinnamon and stir. Spoon over Honey Roasted Chicken to serve.

Chapter 10

Gluten-Free Cuisine

*I will be fully satisfied as with the richest of foods;
with singing lips my mouth will praise you.*

Psalm 63:5

Simple Mexican Horchata and Fruity Taco Wraps

Simple Mexican Horchata

INGREDIENTS:

8 cups rice milk
1 vanilla bean, slit with sharp knife
½ cup sugar
2 cinnamon sticks

DIRECTIONS:

1. Pour rice milk into slow cooker. Add vanilla bean, sugar, and cinnamon sticks. Cover and cook on low for 1 to 2 hours, or until heated through.

2. Ladle into mugs and serve with a cinnamon stick to garnish, if desired.

This is a simple recipe based on a traditional Mexican beverage. Kids will love sipping this while the grownups are having coffee, and you can enjoy it as a warm drink before bed!

Fruity Taco Wraps

INGREDIENTS:

8 gluten-free corn tortillas
16 oz. plain yogurt
2 tsp. vanilla
½ cup blueberries
½ cup pineapple chunks
½ cup sliced peaches
½ cup sliced mango

DIRECTIONS:

1. In large bowl, stir together yogurt and vanilla. Add blueberries, pineapple, peaches, and mango. Toss gently to combine.

2. Spoon yogurt mixture into tortillas. Secure seam with toothpick and place in slow cooker.

3. Cover and cook on low for 2 to 3 hours.

I'm always on the lookout for healthy and delicious after-school snacks for my kids, and this one's a winner!

Vegetarian Green Peppers and Almond Torte

Vegetarian Green Peppers

INGREDIENTS:

3 green bell peppers
1 15-oz. can pinto beans, rinsed and drained
1 cup corn
1 cup cooked rice
1½ tsp. cumin
2 cloves garlic, minced
1 tsp. chili powder
2 oz. grated cheddar cheese
1 Tbsp. fresh cilantro, chopped
¼ cup water

DIRECTIONS:

1. Cut peppers in half lengthwise and remove seeds.

2. In a large bowl, combine beans, corn, rice, cumin, garlic, and chili powder. Spoon mixture into each pepper and place in greased slow cooker.

3. Pour water around peppers into bottom of slow cooker. Cover and cook on low for 5 to 6 hours.

4. Top peppers with cheddar and cilantro. Cover and cook for an additional 30 minutes.

Almond Torte

INGREDIENTS:

6 eggs, separated
1 cup sugar, divided
1½ cups crushed almonds, plus ¼ cup sliced almonds
1 cup leftover mashed potatoes
1 lemon

DIRECTIONS:

1. In medium bowl, beat the egg yolks until light and lemon-colored. Gradually add ½ cup sugar, a small amount at a time. Continue beating for approximately 10 minutes.

2. Squeeze the lemon and grate rind. Add juice and 1 tsp. zest to the eggs. Stir in crushed almonds and mashed potatoes. Beat until well blended.

3. In a separate bowl, beat the egg whites until stiff. Gradually add the remaining ½ cup of sugar. Continue beating until the egg whites are stiff but not dry. Fold whites into the yolk mixture and pour into slow cooker. Scatter sliced almonds over top.

4. Cover and cook on high for 2 hours.

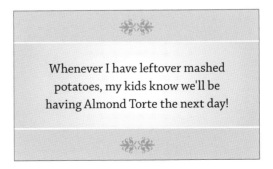

Whenever I have leftover mashed potatoes, my kids know we'll be having Almond Torte the next day!

Apple Upside-Down Cake

INGREDIENTS:

¼ cup butter
1 cup brown sugar
½ cup white sugar, divided
8 apples, peeled, cored, and chopped
½ cup chopped walnuts
Juice of 1 lemon, freshly squeezed
5 eggs, separated
1 tsp. lemon juice
¼ cup gluten-free potato starch, sifted

DIRECTIONS:

1. Create a foil sling by lining slow cooker with aluminum foil. Foil should come at least six inches up the sides of the slow cooker. Grease well.

2. Melt butter in small saucepan. Stir in brown sugar, then pour into bottom of slow cooker. Sprinkle the walnuts over top and scatter apples over nuts. Pour lemon juice over apples.

3. In a separate bowl beat egg yolks with ½ cup sugar until very light. Add lemon juice and sifted potato starch to the egg yolk mixture and stir until moist.

4. In a separate bowl, beat the egg whites until stiff but not dry. Carefully fold the beaten egg whites into the egg yolk mixture. Pour the batter over the apples. Cover and cook on low for 3 to 4 hours, or until a toothpick inserted in the center comes out clean.

5. Grasp foil sling and lift cake out of slow cooker. Carefully flip onto cake plate and remove foil sling. Let cool before serving.

Lemon Chicken on Quinoa

INGREDIENTS:

6 boneless, skinless chicken breasts
1⅓ cups uncooked quinoa
¼ cup brown sugar
2 tsp. vinegar
3 Tbsp. ketchup
1 small onion, minced
1 cup lemonade concentrate
6 Tbsp. water, divided
2 Tbsp. cornstarch

DIRECTIONS:

1. Put quinoa in bottom of slow cooker and lay chicken on top.

2. In small bowl, mix together brown sugar, vinegar, ketchup, onion, lemonade concentrate, and ¼ cup water. Stir together cornstarch and remaining 2 Tbsp. water in small bowl, then stir into lemonade mixture.

3. Pour lemonade mixture over chicken. Cover and cook on low for 6 hours.

Sloppy Beans and Comfort Tapioca Pudding

Sloppy Beans

INGREDIENTS:

1 lb. ground beef
½ cup tomato sauce
1 small onion, chopped
¼ cup ketchup
1 green bell pepper, seeded and chopped
1 Tbsp. apple cider vinegar
1 celery stalk, chopped
1 Tbsp. brown sugar
1 tsp. salt
2 28-oz. cans baked beans

DIRECTIONS:

1. Brown hamburger in skillet. Drain grease and transfer meat to slow cooker.

2. Add all other ingredients to the slow cooker and mix well. Cover and cook on low for 6 to 8 hours.

These beans are good on anything—
over rice cakes, as a side dish, on
top of hot dogs—everything!

Comfort Tapioca Pudding

INGREDIENTS:

2 cups milk
1 cup heavy cream
1 tsp. vanilla
⅛ tsp. salt
½ cup small pearl tapioca
2 eggs, lightly beaten
⅓ cup sugar
Fresh berries

A little bit goes a long way with this rich pudding, but you'll be smacking your lips for a long time!

DIRECTIONS:

1. Stir together the milk, cream, vanilla, salt, and tapioca in slow cooker. Cover and cook on high for 2 hours, stirring occasionally.

2. In a small bowl, whisk together the eggs and sugar. Add 2 Tbsp. tapioca to bowl and stir to combine, then add egg mixture to slow cooker. Cover and cook on high for 15 minutes, stirring once.

3. Let cool at room temperature, then transfer to refrigerator. Serve chilled with fresh berries scattered over each portion.

Lime Chili Roasted Carrots and Sausage Casserole

Lime Chili Roasted Carrots

INGREDIENTS:

- 10 carrots, peeled and chopped
- 1½ tsp. chili powder
- Juice of 1 lime, freshly squeezed
- 1 tsp. salt
- 1 tsp. freshly ground black pepper
- 3 Tbsp. olive oil
- 1 tsp. grated lime zest

DIRECTIONS:

1. Add carrots to slow cooker and toss with chili powder, lime juice, salt, pepper, and olive oil.

2. Cover and cook on low for 4 to 5 hours. Sprinkle with lime zest just before serving.

Sausage Casserole

INGREDIENTS:

5 red bliss potatoes, sliced thin
1 small onion, chopped
1 lb. ground sausage, browned
2 Tbsp. butter, melted
1 tsp. dried basil
1 tsp. dried oregano
½ tsp. dried parsley
1 tsp. salt
½ tsp. pepper

DIRECTIONS:

1. Grease slow cooker and arrange layers of potato slices on the bottom.

2. In small bowl, combine melted butter with basil, oregano, parsley, salt, and pepper. Pour over potatoes.

3. Mix together sausage and onion. Spoon into slow cooker over potatoes.

4. Cover and cook on high for 3 to 4 hours.

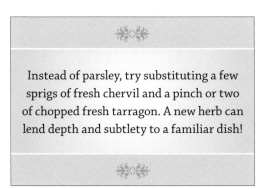

Instead of parsley, try substituting a few sprigs of fresh chervil and a pinch or two of chopped fresh tarragon. A new herb can lend depth and subtlety to a familiar dish!

Cheesy Burgers

INGREDIENTS:

1 lb. ground beef
1 tsp. salt
1 tsp. pepper
½ tsp. garlic powder
2 baking potatoes, sliced thin
6 slices cheddar cheese
6 rice cakes
To serve: ketchup, mustard, relish, sliced red onions, tomatoes, and lettuce

DIRECTIONS:

1. Line bottom of slow cooker with sliced potatoes.

2. In large bowl, mix together ground beef, salt, pepper, and garlic powder. Shape into patties and place on top of potatoes in slow cooker. Place a fork between the pot and the lid and cook on high for 90 minutes.

3. Top each patty with a slice of cheese. Cook an additional 15 minutes, or until melted.

4. Remove hamburgers and discard grease-soaked potatoes. Serve hamburgers on rice cakes with desired condiments.

Molten Lava Pudding

INGREDIENTS:

1 16-oz. box gluten-free brownie mix
¼ cup vegetable oil
1 egg, beaten
¼ cup water
1 14-oz. can sweetened condensed milk
Vanilla ice cream for serving (optional)

DIRECTIONS:

1. In a mixing bowl, combine the brownie mix, oil, egg, water, and sweetened condensed milk.

2. Cover and cook on low for 3 to 4 hours, stirring occasionally. Serve warm over vanilla ice cream.

Golden Ring Pheasant and Four Fruit Wild Rice

Golden Ring Pheasant

INGREDIENTS:

- 1 golden ring pheasant
- 8 oz. raspberry vinaigrette
- ½ tsp. freshly ground black pepper
- ½ tsp. salt
- ½ tsp. paprika
- ¼ tsp. cloves
- ¼ tsp. nutmeg
- ½ tsp. cardamom

DIRECTIONS:

1. Marinate pheasant in raspberry vinaigrette overnight.

2. In small bowl, mix together pepper, salt, paprika, cloves, nutmeg, and cardamom. Place pheasant in slow cooker and sprinkle spice mixture over top. Cover and cook on low for 7 to 8 hours.

Most grocery stores carry pheasant, but if you can't find it substitute a whole chicken.

Four Fruit Wild Rice

INGREDIENTS:

½ cup uncooked wild rice
2 qts. water
½ cup dried cranberries
½ cup golden raisins
½ cup dried cherries
½ cup dried blueberries
2 green onions, finely chopped
Juice of 3 limes, freshly squeezed
½ cup sugar
2 Tbsp. apple cider vinegar
1 Tbsp. olive oil
1 cup hazelnuts

DIRECTIONS:

1. Combine wild rice and water in a medium saucepan. Bring to a boil, then reduce to simmer and cook until tender, about 25 minutes. Drain and transfer to slow cooker.

2. Add cranberries, raisins, cherries, blueberries, green onions, lime juice, sugar, vinegar, and olive oil to slow cooker. Stir well to combine. Cover and cook on low for 5 to 6 hours.

3. In the meantime, preheat oven to 350°. Put hazelnuts on rimmed baking sheet and roast 5 to 10 minutes.

4. Fluff rice with fork and garnish with hazelnuts to serve.

Honey-Dijon Brussels Sprouts

INGREDIENTS:

1 lb. Brussels sprouts
1 Tbsp. honey Dijon mustard
2 cloves fresh garlic, peeled and minced
1 Tbsp. olive oil
1 tsp. salt
1 tsp. freshly ground pepper
¼ cup water

DIRECTIONS:

1. Put Brussels sprouts in slow cooker.

2. In small bowl, combine mustard, garlic, olive oil, salt, pepper, and water. Pour over Brussels sprouts and toss to coat.

3. Cover and cook on low for 4 hours. Serve with sauce spooned over.

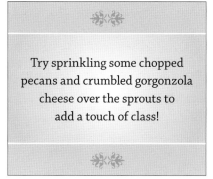

Try sprinkling some chopped pecans and crumbled gorgonzola cheese over the sprouts to add a touch of class!

Veggie Meatloaf

INGREDIENTS:

½ cup almond milk
1 cup cornmeal
2 lbs. ground turkey
3 egg whites, beaten
1 stalk celery, chopped
1 large carrot, peeled and grated
1 small zucchini, grated
1 green bell pepper, seeded and chopped
¼ cup sundried tomatoes, chopped fine
¼ cup brown sugar, divided
½ cup tomato sauce

DIRECTIONS:

1. Combine almond milk, cornmeal, turkey, egg whites, celery, carrot, zucchini, pepper, sundried tomatoes, and 2 Tbsp. brown sugar in a large mixing bowl. Blend thoroughly with hands and shape into loaf.

2. Set loaf in slow cooker. Cover and cook on low for 5 hours.

3. Mix remaining 2 Tbsp. brown sugar and tomato sauce in a small bowl. Pour the tomato sauce mixture on top of meatloaf. Cover and cook on high for 1 to 2 additional hours.

4. To serve, remove loaf to serving platter.

Beef with Horseradish and Kansas Corn Pudding

Beef with Horseradish

INGREDIENTS:

4 8-oz. steaks
1 small onion, sliced thin
2 Tbsp. butter
1 tsp. salt
1 tsp. freshly ground pepper
2 Tbsp. soy sauce
½ cup white grape juice
1 cup sour cream
2 tsp. prepared horseradish
2 tsp. chopped fresh dill

DIRECTIONS:

1. Melt butter in large skillet set over medium heat. Add steaks and onion. Cook steaks until brown, 3 to 5 minutes per side. Transfer meat and onions to slow cooker.

2. Add salt, pepper, soy sauce, and white grape juice to slow cooker. Cover and cook on low for 4 hours.

3. In small bowl, combine sour cream, horseradish, and dill. Pour over steaks, then cover and cook for 30 minutes.

Kansas Corn Pudding

INGREDIENTS:

4 eggs
3 cups corn kernels, drained
2 tsp. fresh grated onion
3 Tbsp. sweet rice flour
½ tsp. salt
2 Tbsp. sugar
¼ tsp. cayenne pepper
¼ tsp. ground nutmeg
¼ cup butter, melted
1½ cups half-and-half

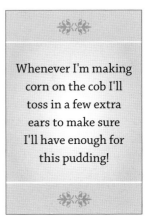

Whenever I'm making corn on the cob I'll toss in a few extra ears to make sure I'll have enough for this pudding!

DIRECTIONS:

1. In a large mixing bowl beat eggs with an electric mixer until frothy, then stir in the corn and onion.

2. In a small bowl combine rice flour, salt, sugar, cayenne, and nutmeg. Stir into the corn mixture, then add the melted butter and half-and-half.

3. Pour into greased slow cooker.

4. Cover and cook on low for 5 to 6 hours.

Italian Beef Sandwiches and Mocha Tofu Cake

Italian Beef Sandwiches

INGREDIENTS:

1 5-lb. rump roast
1 tsp. freshly ground black pepper
1 tsp. dried oregano
1 tsp. dried basil
1 tsp. onion salt
1 tsp. dried parsley
1 tsp. garlic powder
1 bay leaf
8 oz. hot or mild giardiniera relish, plus additional for serving
6 rice cakes

DIRECTIONS:

1. Place meat in slow cooker. Add 4 to 6 cups water until the meat is almost covered.

2. Add pepper, oregano, basil, onion, salt, parsley, garlic powder, and bay leaf to slow cooker. Stir in giardiniera relish. Cover and cook on high for 4 to 5 hours.

3. Remove bay leaf. Shred beef with two forks, leaving meat in liquid. Spoon over rice cakes to serve, topping with additional giardiniera relish.

Mocha Tofu Cake

INGREDIENTS:

8 oz. silken tofu
¼ cup ricotta cheese
4 oz. cream cheese
¼ cup real maple syrup
3 Tbsp. unsweetened cocoa powder
2 egg whites, beaten
1 Tbsp. ground cinnamon
¼ cup strong coffee

DIRECTIONS:

1. Combine all ingredients in large mixing bowl using electric beaters. Mix until smooth, then pour into greased slow cooker.

2. Cover and cook on low for 2 to 3 hours, making sure not to overcook. Slice cake and serve.

Book Club Chai Tea and
Lady Love Deviled Egg Dip

Book Club Chai Tea

INGREDIENTS:

8 cups water
4 black tea bags
½ cup honey
10 whole cloves
4 cinnamon sticks
1 cup half-and-half
1 tsp. vanilla

DIRECTIONS:

1. Combine water, tea, honey, cloves, and cinnamon sticks in slow cooker. Cover and cook on high for 2 to 3 hours.

2. Strain, discarding tea bags, cloves, and cinnamon sticks. Stir in half-and-half and vanilla. Cover and cook 30 additional minutes, or until heated through.

3. Ladle into mugs and serve with a fresh cinnamon stick at the next meeting of your book club.

Lady Love Deviled Egg Dip

INGREDIENTS:

12 eggs
6 Tbsp. mayonnaise
1 Tbsp. sugar
½ cup dill relish
2 tsp. prepared horseradish
1 tsp. prepared mustard
1 tsp. salt
1 tsp. freshly ground black pepper
1 Tbsp. fresh parsley, chopped

DIRECTIONS:

1. Place eggs in large saucepan in single layer. Add cold water to cover by at least 1 inch.

2. Cover and heat water to boiling. Remove pan from heat and let stand 20 minutes. Crack shells by tapping gently all over, then rolling between hands to loosen.

3. Cut eggs in half lengthwise. Scoop out yolk and transfer to small bowl. Set whites aside. Mash yolks with fork. Stir mayonnaise, sugar, relish, horseradish, mustard, salt, and pepper into yolks.

4. Chop egg whites into small pieces. Stir whites into yolk mixture. Transfer mixture to slow cooker, cover, and cook on low for 2 to 3 hours.

5. Sprinkle fresh parsley on Deviled Egg Dip. Serve as a hot dip with cut beets, baby carrots, cut cucumbers, cauliflower, broccoli, cherry tomatoes, sugar snap peas, and sliced bell peppers.

Cornbread-Stuffed Cornish Hens and Mustard Vegetables

Cornbread

INGREDIENTS:

4 eggs
3 cups buttermilk
1 cup sour cream
2 Tbsp. vegetable oil
4 cups yellow cornmeal
pepper
1 Tbsp. onion powder

2 Tbsp. baking soda
2 tsp. dried sage
1½ tsp. salt
1 Tbsp. sugar
1 tsp. freshly ground black

DIRECTIONS:

1. In large mixing bowl, beat eggs, buttermilk, sour cream, and oil with a fork. In separate bowl, toss all dry ingredients until blended. Stir dry mixture into buttermilk mixture until just blended. Pour batter into greased slow cooker.

2. Cover and cook on high for 1 hour. Cornbread is done when edges are brown and pull away from sides. Remove and cool on wire rack.

3. Cut cornbread in half. Use one half for stuffing recipe, serving the rest with dinner.

Cornbread-Stuffed Cornish Hens

INGREDIENTS:

½ cup butter, divided
1 large Vidalia onion, coarsely chopped
1 cup celery, diced
½ cup parsley, chopped
½ cornbread recipe, crumbled
½ cup dried cranberries

¼ cup gluten-free chicken broth, preferably homemade
4 Cornish hens

DIRECTIONS:

1. Melt 4 Tbsp. butter in skillet set over medium heat. Add onion and sauté until golden, about 15 minutes. Add celery and sauté 10 more minutes. Remove from heat and stir in parsley. Set aside to cool.

2. Crumble cornbread into a large mixing bowl. Stir in cranberries and onion mixture. Melt remaining 4 Tbsp. butter and drizzle over stuffing, tossing lightly. Sprinkle with broth and mix lightly again. Stuff mixture inside hens.

3. Cover and cook on high for 3 to 4 hours. Hens are done when a meat thermometer reaches 160°.

Mustard Vegetables

INGREDIENTS:

1 lb. baby carrots
1 lb. broccoli florets,
1 lb. fresh cauliflower florets, chopped big
1 cup brown sugar
½ cup honey Dijon mustard
2 Tbsp. gluten-free soy sauce

DIRECTIONS:

1. Combine carrots, broccoli, and cauliflower in slow cooker.

2. In a separate bowl, mix brown sugar, mustard, and soy sauce. Pour over vegetables and toss to coat. Cover and cook on low for 4 to 6 hours.

INDEX

269